PRAISE FOR
LEAN STARTUP,
LEAN COMPANY,
RICH EXIT

Dr. Kenan Sahin's 2024 book *Lean Startup, to Lean Company, to Rich Exit* is a fascinating and compelling story of success by a serial entrepreneur and one of the most successful graduates of MIT. He took a one-person consulting firm and built it into a powerhouse in the telecommunications space, overcoming all of the established players. This guidebook is a companion to his earlier book and extends it with a comprehensive framework for practical use by aspiring entrepreneurs. It starts with a big-picture perspective: the importance of having multiple projects under way and the importance of building professional networks to drive innovation. Then, it moves on to specific and actionable advice that new entrepreneurs need to know: how to hire the best people; how to provide incentives through bonuses and profit sharing; how to handle billing and invoices; how to hire a good lawyer; compensation plans for sales staff; and even, how to negotiate leases for office space.

—Dr. Keith Sawyer
The Morgan Distinguished Professor in Educational Innovations at the University of North Carolina at Chapel Hill

Author of Group Genius: The Creative Power of Collaboration *and* Zig Zag: The Surprising Path to Greater Creativity

In his deeply insightful memoir, *Lean Startup, to Lean Company, to Rich Exit*, Kenan Sahin tells the story of building a company from a $1,000 seedling to one of the most lucrative sales in the US, filling the book with insightful anecdotes and hard-won lessons for navigating the long road to success. In this follow-up guidebook, Sahin drills down into practical lessons and first principles to lay out a roadmap that other entrepreneurs can readily follow. It is rich with first-hand advice from starting up to facing the formidable challenges of when and how to grow and diversify—and, just as importantly, what to do when you succeed.

—Bob Buderi

Former Editor in Chief, MIT Technology Review

Author, Where Futures Converge: Kendall Square and the Making of a Global Innovation Hub

LEAN STARTUP, LEAN COMPANY, RICH EXIT

KENAN E. SAHIN, PhD
with Kent E. Sahin

LEAN STARTUP, LEAN COMPANY, RICH EXIT

→

The Guidebook

AN ACADEMIC ENTREPRENEUR'S GUIDE TO NAVIGATING
THE "VALLEY OF DEATH" AND SURVIVING THE EVEN MORE
TREACHEROUS "GREEN VALLEYS" ON THE WAY TO THE TOP

Forbes | Books

Published by Forbes Books, Charleston, South Carolina.
An imprint of Advantage Media Group.

Forbes Books is a registered trademark, and the Forbes Books colophon is a trademark of Forbes Media, LLC.

Printed in the United States of America.

10 9 8 7 6 5 4 3 2 1

ISBN: 979-8-88750-251-9 (Hardcover)
ISBN: 979-8-88750-647-0 (Paperback)
ISBN: 979-8-88750-252-6 (eBook)

Library of Congress Control Number: 2024918472

Cover design by Matthew Morse.
Layout design by Lance Buckley.

This custom publication is intended to provide accurate information and the opinions of the author in regard to the subject matter covered. It is sold with the understanding that the publisher, Forbes Books, is not engaged in rendering legal, financial, or professional services of any kind. If legal advice or other expert assistance is required, the reader is advised to seek the services of a competent professional.

Since 1917, Forbes has remained steadfast in its mission to serve as the defining voice of entrepreneurial capitalism. Forbes Books, launched in 2016 through a partnership with Advantage Media, furthers that aim by helping business and thought leaders bring their stories, passion, and knowledge to the forefront in custom books. Opinions expressed by Forbes Books authors are their own. To be considered for publication, please visit **books.Forbes.com**.

To MIT for educating me at the frontiers of knowledge as a whole person; those MIT Sloan Fellows who were my students, for teaching me far more than I taught them; the Fellows who after graduating guided me in the field and presented Kenan Systems with incredible challenges; Howard Johnson, Jerome Wiesner, and Charles Vest, all MIT presidents, who graciously served on the boards of Kenan Systems (Johnson, Wiesner) and TIAX (Vest) and who continuously inspired me and were the ultimate check and balance during my tenure as president.

To colleagues at Kenan Systems, Lucent, and Bell Labs for the incredible journey we shared, validating and creating many guideposts from a lean startup to a rich exit that was a culmination at Lucent and Bell Labs.

And of course, to my family, for not just watching me but being an integral part of these journeys, especially my sons.

CONTENTS

INTRODUCTION

Why start your own company when there are plenty out there already?

If everyone went out and started their own company, there'd be nobody left to work for any of these startups.

On the other hand, if everyone went to work for existing companies, that would lead to economic stagnation or worse—a continuing corporate consolidation that left the commercial landscape with but a few monster-sized companies.

So, the pendulum swings, though historically it has not been so much a pendulum but a spiral.

At each winding of the spiral, a population of startups rises to become larger companies capable of pushing the legacy giants off into history. Call it the capitalist renewal project. This spiraling dynamic allows for a more rapid conversion of new ideas, inventions, and technologies from new players capable of accelerating progress—hopefully for the betterment of us all.

Of course, all this spiraling upward and outward is a macro concept. It is a churn of societal aspirations, market ambitions, and government directives—whatever they may be. As for the individual looking to begin a company, that action is instead driven by very micro motivations:

- Taking an invention to market
- Making a lot of money

- Not getting rich, but gaining financial independence
- Pursuing a passion
- Becoming your own boss
- Giving back
- Building a lasting legacy
- Positively impacting one of society's big challenges
- Having the freedom to work from anywhere
- Being with others of similar interests
- Putting food on the table
- Leaving a job you hate for one that couldn't be worse
- It's in your blood, and you must

Some **startuppers**, if I may call them that, might love the thrill of cranking up a new engine for the first time, but they soon lose interest and move on to the next engine.

Others might enjoy the journey to the next stop and happily disembark. For them, attaining a stable level of business is good enough, and they are happy to exit it or let it run—either way—for they have built a great business.

Still others might want their startup to become a viable, sustainable company and then achieve a **Rich Exit** with a big, lasting impact.

Whatever your own end game, how to get going?

We are in an era awash with venture capital, and in the right sectors with the right pitches, venture capitalists are eager to throw money at entrepreneurs. So, untold thousands of entrepreneurs can start out rich and hopefully then achieve a **Rich Exit**. Of course, these venture capitalists are usually investing other people's money and are looking to earn outsize returns given the big risks involved. So, they sprinkle cash into as many startups as they can keep track of, then swiftly weed out all who do not produce quick revenues and a path to a sale. This can be the best or worst of all approaches for a founder to take.

There is another approach to this, one that I followed, tested in the field, and will describe here as an implementable guide.

That approach is to create a very **lean-running startup**, preferably using your own funds, evolve the startup into a still **lean, sustainable company**, and then grow it for a big impact. At that point, the choice becomes to remain involved with the company but with duties scaled back (a form of **Rich Exit**) or sell it outright for a substantial price that signifies a truly **Rich Exit**.

The journey from start to exit is complex, full of mousetraps on up to elephant traps spread across a lot of uncharted territory. Until a level of toughness and resilience is finally attained, the journey is a lot like driving along a narrow and winding unmarked mountain road in a hailstorm at night.

My Motivation, My Background

I had been a professor for nearly a decade and a half, teaching undergraduates and graduate students at MIT, Harvard, and the University of Massachusetts in Amherst, as well as midlevel executives coming for a master's degree at MIT. My teaching stints had always been highly rated, and I was even given the Salgo-Noren Teaching Excellence Award.[1] However, a niggling bit of self-doubt had crept in, and I couldn't ignore it. The reason?

I didn't know if all the things I was telling my students made any sense at all—for I had never worked in what we call "the real world." Not even for a minute. How valid was the content of my teaching? Was I just telling stories? Just winging it on my charm and good looks? (Even I knew better than that!)

---

1   The Salgo-Noren Foundation, https://salgotrust.org/about.

It became clear that as my students scattered to the winds that I, too, needed to do some scattering. Needed to go out and validate my academic theories, postulations, and pontifications about expert systems, big data-based information systems, and, more broadly, the precise ways in which technology could be used to engineer a better-functioning organization.

Why not start a company and find out?

Why not go out and do legitimate field validation?

So, that became my primary motivation for going into business: to move my experiment from the lab to the real world. A simple experiment it would not be, however. It would become a seventeen-year journey from **Lean Startup** to **Lean Company** to **Rich Exit**.

What Happened Seventeen Years Later

I chronicled that journey in the first book in this series, *Lean Startup to Lean Company to Rich Exit*. Here's an excerpt from the prologue summarizing what happened:

> *January 26, 1999. News outlets in Boston and around the world announced in bold headlines that **Kenan Systems Corporation** had been sold to Lucent Technologies for $1.54 billion in stock, all paid up front without any caveats or golden handcuffs on the company founder who was free to walk the next day. The stock was convertible to cash after only 30 days.*
>
> *Only thirteen deals were larger in a year for acquisitions that saw 10,892 of them in the US, and this was the only deal of this magnitude where the founder was also the sole shareholder, quite unprecedented.*
>
> *I am Kenan Sahin, that founder and CEO. This book is about Kenan Systems being launched as a Lean Startup with $1,000, evolving into a Lean Company, and seventeen years later achieving a Rich Exit.*

Also unprecedented was Lucent, which owned and operated Bell Labs, agreeing to hire the 700 technical staff of Kenan Systems as Members of Bell Labs Staff, a highly coveted position in the century-old crown jewel of American research and development.

Kenan Systems had built several early artificial intelligence (AI) and big data systems and parlayed those into its marquee product, the ARBOR Telecommunications Billing and Customer Care Platform that today services more than a billion telecom customers or about a third of the global subscribers.

Why This Series of Books

It's all about innovation, really. I am all for innovation but much more so for its implementation in the marketplace for the benefit of society, the myriads of people who take innovations to implementation, and of course the innovators.

When you look at how much money is spent on innovation, it's rather eye opening. All governments around the world are keen on seeding business innovation, but that practice defies comparison in the US. From 2022 to 2024, the average US government allotment to R&D was $210 billion; industry added $600 billion for companies' internal R&D efforts, nonprofits and universities added another $50 billion, and venture capitalists brought $200 billion to the table for a grand—very grand—total well above a trillion dollars, or about 4 percent of the country's GDP.[2]

---

2   "Federal Research and Development (R&D) Funding: FY2024," Congressional Research Service, May 19, 2023, https://crsreports.congress.gov/product/pdf/R/R47564; "Business R&D Performance in the United States Tops $600 Billion in 2021," National Center for Science and Engineering Statistics and Census Bureau, September 28, 2023, https://ncses.nsf.gov/pubs/nsf23350; "R&D Expenditures at US Universities Increased by $8 Billion in FY 2022," National Center for Science and Engineering Statistics, November 30, 2023, https://ncses.nsf.gov/pubs/nsf24307; Barbara Tague, "Venture Capital Trends and Outlook for 2024," AlphaSense, April 29, 2024, https://www.alpha-sense.com/blog/trends/venture-capital-trends-outlook/.

U.S. R&D FUNDING BY SOURCE
(average annual for 2022-2024 period)

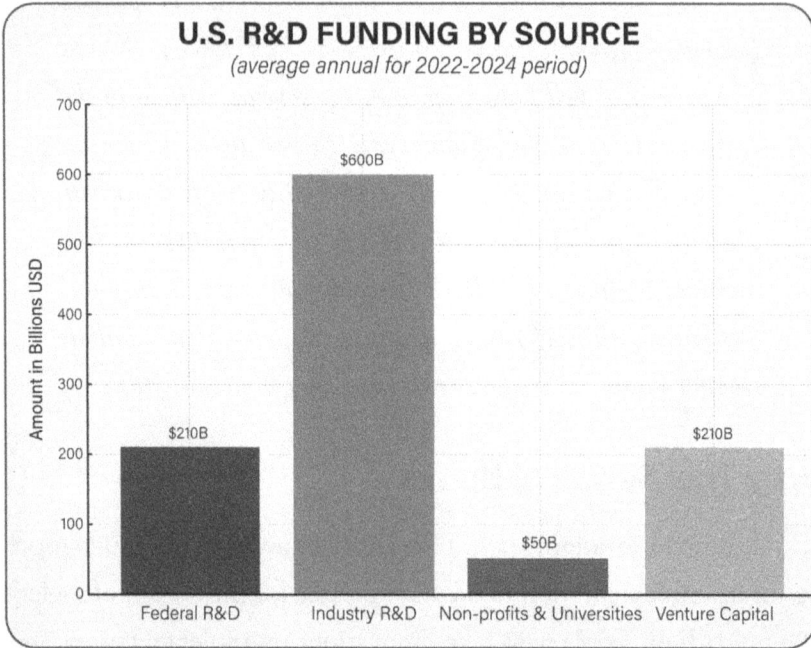

Figure 0.1. Total US R&D spending between 2022
and 2024 has surpassed a trillion dollars.

These vast sums of R&D funds are dispersed to universities as well as innovation-driven startups popping up in every city with supporting infrastructure. Venture capitalists seek out every capable entrepreneur with their siren calls, allowing none to strap themselves to the mast. The innovation engines are roaring with literally millions of startups being founded every year.

It should all be wonderful.

Except that the implementation engines—the machinery that takes all these innovations from the lab to market—have remained largely static entities. And this has resulted in a massive **innovation backlog**.

As a business community, we're failing on the critical metrics.

STARTUP TO IPO WINNOWING

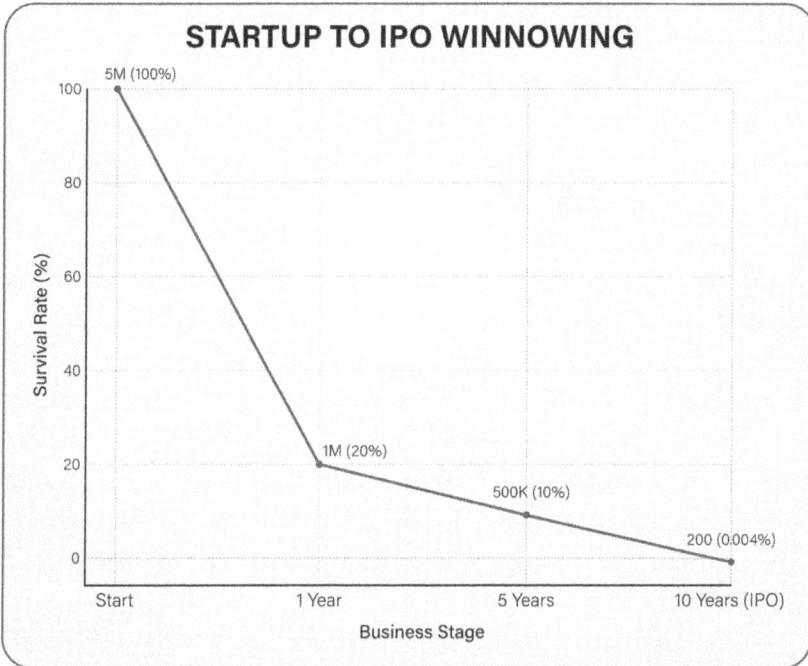

Figure 0.2. *The winnowing from startup to IPO gives companies a 1 in 25,000 chance of a Rich Exit.*

Take the startup environment of today. The Census Bureau tells us that some five million new business applications are filed every year now, up nearly 100 percent from a decade ago.[3] Statista tells us that fewer than one million companies are one year or less old.[4] So, roughly one out of five make it through the first year. And by year five, that drops to one in ten.

This winnowing then gets even more brutal. In 2022, there were about two hundred IPOs, which is close to the average annual

---

3   "Business Formation Statistics," Census.gov, n.d., https://www.census.gov/econ/bfs/index.html.

4   "Number of business establishments, by age, US 2022," Statista, February 14, 2023: https://www.statista.com/statistics/873316/number-of-entrepreneurial-businesses-in-the-us-by-age/.

number.[5] This means that just about one in twenty-five thousand startups make it all the way to a **Rich Exit**.

Tracking these **Rich Exits** even further and looking out beyond the IPO a few years, more than half are underwater.[6] They are either losing money or underperforming, and innovations are not coming to market like they should.

This alarming news has actually gotten worse in recent years.

Back in the mid-1990s, there were 7,322 companies listed on major US stock exchanges at a time when the US population was 266 million.[7] That means there were about twenty-eight listed companies for every one million citizens. That was the peak. By 2023, the number of public companies dropped to 5,860 while the population hit 332 million. That works out to about eighteen companies per million citizens. Other things factor in, of course, but the net takeaway is this: despite three decades of a feverish-paced IPO market, public companies are on a serious decline.

How about the merger and acquisition (M&A) market? Is it contributing?

M&A deals in the US tend to add up to between 10,000 and 14,000 per year, with a total deal value of around $2 trillion.[8] Actual value totals can skew year to year because of megadeals—such as the 2021 acquisition of Kansas City Southern by Canadian Pacific Railway for $33.6 billion, creating the first rail network from Canada to Mexico.[9] But if we focus in on these M&A stats, looking at **Rich**

---

5   "Number of IPOs in the US 1999–2022," Statista, February 3, 2023, https://www.statista.com/statistics/270290/number-of-ipos-in-the-us-since-1999/.

6   Kerry Sun, "Half of All 2021 IPOs Underwater after Record Year for Listings," Market Index, December 31, 2021, https://www.marketindex.com.au/news/half-of-all-2021-ipos-underwater-after-record-year-for-listings.

7   Based on data compiled from the World Federation of Exchanges and the Census Bureau.

8   "Number of M&A deals in the US 2020–2022, by deal value," Statista, May 22, 2023, https://www.statista.com/statistics/245977/number-of-munda-deals-in-the-united-states/.

9   "Canadian Pacific and Kansas City Southern Combination Approved by US Surface Transportation Board," Kansas City Southern, March 15, 2023, https://www.kcsouthern.com/media/news/news-releases/canadian-pacific-and-kansas-city-southern-combination-approved-by-u-s-surface-transportation-board.

Exits totaling $1 billion or more, we find that on average only ten startups a year make it to that fabled unicorn status.[10]

I am a great supporter of innovations and the startups that carry those into the marketplace. Imagine a world in which the winnowing of 25,000 startups to only one IPO goes up to ten or even one hundred IPO's. And the listed companies jump from the paltry 6,000 companies or so to 60,000 and even more.

The impact would be remarkable.

Can it be done? I believe so. And I believe it should be so. But it will require a web of policies, guidance, collaboration, and healthy (not predatory) competition.

With some bias and partiality I will highlight the MIT ecosystem as a proof point as it has achieved success far above the averages. As described In the book *Entrepreneurship and Innovation at MIT by Ed Roberts, Fiona Murray, et al* as of 2014 there were 30,200 MIT alumni founded active companies, employing 4.6 million people and generating nearly two trillion in revenue, equivalent to the economies (in gross domestic product terms) of Italy or Canada or S. Korea.

What if such ecosystems were the rule rather than the exception?

A key starting point for such a massive expansion in the success rate is the startup itself. For it to succeed, as Kenan Systems did, a long string of independent events need to turn out absolutely right. We can allow, correctly, that luck always plays a big role in success. Nonetheless ...

If this long string of independent events is handled well and principles of success are iterated, then the outcome is more predictably put into the hands of the founders.

My first book outlined the principles I used to guide Kenan Systems through its seventeen years. These principles helped us navigate what many entrepreneurs call the "Valley of Death"—the risky period of cash deficits in a startup's early days, preceding actual revenue from products or services—and emerge on the other side. Its scope took readers from **Lean Startup** to **Lean Company** to **Rich Exit**.

---

10   Alex Lazarow, "Beyond Silicon Valley," Harvard Business Review, March–April 2020, https://hbr.org/2020/03/beyond-silicon-valley.

Many of those principles and anecdotal side trips in that book apply directly to any startup today—from day one through to the end game.

In this second book, I am re-presenting these first principles in a much more practical format for implementation. Think of it as an academic entrepreneur aiming to drill down on what has worked, and why it can again for you.

This is meant to be a stand-alone work that's easy to reference as needed since it is organized along the progression from startup to sizable company to potential **Rich Exit.** If you elect to read the first book first, you'll get more of a context and may amuse yourself with the more dramatic moments we faced at Kenan Systems. You may even see reflections of what's ahead for you.

As in the first book, these views are solely my own and do not represent the views of any of the organizations I have been affiliated with over the years.

I am hoping that these two volumes increase the odds of success of today's startups and hand in hand reduce the growing backlog of innovations. Without successful implementation, these innovations are like bountiful produce on farms doomed to rot away for lack of transportation to the markets. What a waste of amazing innovations and worse the incredible talents of so many involved in startups.

Not what we want! And what we want can happen. I am hoping these two volumes will be helpful in generating many amazing stories everywhere from Innovation to Implementation to Impact.

PART I

FROM LEAN STARTUP TO LEAN COMPANY

1

LAUNCHING A
LEAN STARTUP

First, a note about the use of the word you *in these pages. You could be a CEO, a management team, a member of a board, or anyone influencing the course of a company. A founder may guide the startup to point A and then relinquish the key role to senior management at point B and then hand off authority to an entire cadre of managers at point C. So, the* you *is truly a composite that evolves. However, when an individual such as a CEO needs to be singled out, it will be done.*

A startup really gets going when you do the work of organizing a portfolio of offers, as I call them. I speak about what we now call a B2B company—business to business. If you are instead looking to launch a consumer products company, your route will still require a portfolio of offers. By *offers*, I mean your talents, products, inventions, business capabilities, or whatever you are offering the market. If you have but a single offer, you will be too narrowly targeted and miss many docking sites, or places it is valued in the market.

You can expect this portfolio of offers to change over time. That's a good thing, a sign of a maturing business. What matters is that the true north sighting of your initial motivations remains in place. That will keep you on track when the oceans of waves that will soon be cresting ahead of you steal the horizon from your view. And steal they will!

Pricing the Offers

Even as the portfolio of offers is assembled, some rudimentary thinking about pricing is important. For the potential customer, if there is interest in an offer, pricing comes into play rather quickly.

If there is inadequate thought given to this, then the offers could be grossly underpriced or overpriced and quickly end a potential sales conversation. Getting the pricing right, or at least the price ranges right, is a critical part of converting offers to orders. So, begin *coupling your offers with rough price ranges.*

Keeping It Lean

The usual next step is to approach a funding group—usually an angel investor—who takes a stake in your promising startup. Since the aim here is to launch as a Lean Startup with you keeping control, let's defer on that.

A key principle to learn and practice over and over right from the get-go is the *art of doing more with less.*

It has always been amazing to me how human ingenuity and creativity can combine in the crucible of the early-stage startup to forge an outsize set of accomplishments. A good example from the 1960s that now seems so distant—so ancient, in fact—involved the early days of cybernetics and computer science. I was an undergrad at MIT then, which meant I was one of those nerds carrying around sleeves of punch cards.

We worked on a mainframe that had a total of 8K core memory. To put this in perspective, that's one hundred times less memory than the app on your cell phone that turns on the little flashlight. But in that spartan computing environment and its equivalents elsewhere, computing languages were already developed such as Fortran to enable large-scale business and scientific applications and LISP to bring expert systems and natural language processing into the marketplace.

Marketing, or Where to Go

If your offers are well articulated, you might first take them to the procurement office of a relevant business and share them. Alas, procurement's job is rarely to buy anything new or innovative. Procurement wants to see product specs, pricing charts, client references, and so on. It's too soon for a Lean Startup.

However, there are people working in these relevant businesses who can be excellent sources of information for the products and services they themselves need. These are the line managers, the back-office people, even the executives who are not in a position to buy directly from you. But they are the ultimate buyers, with procurement acting on their behalf. They are the ones to talk to.

They can be found everywhere.

At industry conferences—where they are the most open to talking.

In associations from the Kiwanis and Lions clubs to industry-specific groups—where they are more relaxed among kindred spirits.

At charity group functions—where their hearts are open and where deep relationships over shared concerns can be naturally forged.

On LinkedIn and industry forums—where they are busy promoting themselves and learning more about their fields of interest.

You want to engage with them as naturally as possible, of course. And in doing so you want to roll out and share the vocabulary that you're building around your portfolio of offers. You're looking to sharpen and reinforce this vocabulary in every relevant conversation, making it more understandable bit by bit until it fully resonates with your audiences.

As these bite-size interactions happen over the weeks and months, several critical things will happen along with them.

You'll learn of the business needs and pain points your prospects are struggling with that you may be able to meet with an offer in your portfolio, or a refined one soon to be there.

You'll learn of your prospect's personal aspirations. It is the individual desires, ambitions, and hidden hopes that each of us has that mean the most to us. That's what drives real demand. Advertising execs know this. They know that aspirations trigger needs, which in turn trigger demand, so they try to gin up aspiration in us. That is the startup's goal as well—to be sought out in every interaction.

This is the seeding phase of business, interacting with people who could become customers, socializing your ideas, getting feedback on them, blending and iterating toward a stronger and stronger set of offers.

When these offers map nicely to your target audience's corporate needs *as well as* their personal aspirations, then it is time to take them formally to potential customers by finding and targeting docking sites.

With a portfolio in hand and rough pricing, start exploring the docking sites for your offers through what I call noisy exploration. The aim here is to *not* confine yourself to well-targeted or scripted market research. And why? Because the world is full of opportunities that at first appear invisible, opportunities that only show themselves once we interact with them, once we begin exploring them, once we tell others about them, and once we get feedback on them. This exploration needs to be richly noisy, though not to the point of being unwieldy. Just enough so that opportunities become visible.

It can be hard for a genuine entrepreneurial type to pull back and put some arbitrary cap on this exploring phase of things. It's in the blood, I think. So, there's great value in knowing instinctively when it's best to stop and declare the portfolio and the target docking sites to be of sufficient variety. Bear in mind that all these processes are iterative. *So, diverge with noisy exploration; converge for focus targeting the identified docking sites.*

These iterations of diverging/converging can be exciting. But again, when's it best to converge? There's no real answer. My own rule of thumb is that when you find that your latest good idea is the same as the one you erased earlier in the search, you've run the course on ideas. But you never know. So, your only real guides can be your intuition and the feedback, sometimes the blowback, that you receive.

Initial engagements secured; now what?

Eventually, and hopefully sooner than later, you'll find an entry point. Your first customer, your first engagement, your first chance at getting paid. Now what? The steps you take here could shape your future (more than you can probably imagine, if you haven't been to this spot before). The first principles that you apply here are, in fact, crucial.

The individual in an organization who welcomes you in might represent your best entry point, an actual bottleneck, or both. That individual is *not* the company but a representative of the company. If that point of entry remains your only gate in, then you are at that person's beck and call, and they are your only channel of communication into the company. So, it's useful to find out who that person's peers are, who reports to them and to whom they report. I call this drawing a circle around the cross.

The horizontal line of the cross is the immediate peers; the vertical line is the immediate superiors and subordinates. Figure out the people who intuitively belong on each arm of the cross and then draw a circle around the cross. That will tell you who you want to meet and network with in the relevant offices of the client organization without getting entangled in their internal dynamics or politics unnecessarily.

This practice protects you from being a captive of your initial contacts in the organization and their ambitions. Rather, by judiciously socializing with those on the cross in the circle, you'll better understand the larger organization's interests. And more, you'll be radiating. That is, you'll be sharing your offer portfolio and rough pricing with surrounding contacts for new opportunities. It's really a powerful combination.

Contracts and the Great IP Lie

Most entrepreneurs wait to figure out all the vagaries of contracts, or plan to call in the lawyers, at the point when a contract *needs* to be drawn up. This can be a glaring mistake. From the very beginning in a Lean Startup, the CEO or founding team needs to know key things about contracts, particularly IP.

A lot of entrepreneurs either willingly or inadvertently hand over the rights to their IP to their early clients, thinking it will cement the relationship. But that can shortchange the company—even if you are a services company and don't have IP-driven product lines. Because you've just given away the future value of your company, at least in the eyes of potential investors.

It happens all the time.

An entrepreneur is drawing up a contract for that very preciously important first contract and is met with these words from the smiling client: "We are paying for this; therefore, whatever IP is generated is ours."

Holding on to IP when doing work for hire is no easy task because the false dogma of "We paid for it; therefore, we own it" is deeply entrenched.

On the surface, this idea seems to make sense, and many entrepreneurs simply accept it. Startups feeling pinched and needing to generate revenue, even if that means entering into less-than-favorable contracts, often succumb to it. Big companies know this.

Big companies enter into a multitude of contracts for goods and services. They naturally, and by that I mean aggressively, push for all they can get. Often this means reaching well beyond what they are actually paying for. These companies want to view these goods and services as "commissioned" or "works for hire." And this is the time when *the great IP lie* card is played.

This is also the time to push back and negotiate.

In fact, payment entitles one to a bundle of rights. What those rights actually entail is a matter to be negotiated and mutually agreed on.

For example, paying for a hotel room for a night entitles one to stay there one night—that is all. Leasing a house for a month is just that—there is no ownership automatically granted. Then there is car buying. No IP ownership comes with the title to the car. Or if it is a lease, the rights are capped (e.g., to miles, to a time period). Full ownership is not automatically granted.

Many entrepreneurs who push back find the big company's fallback position is to propose a compromise: joint ownership. Even that can become a future obstacle while unnecessarily diluting the valuation of the startup.

In my entrepreneurial career, I ended up negotiating hundreds of contracts and encountered *the great IP lie* ad nauseam. In one of the early projects for a very large company, since the funding and the scope were too small for their lawyers to be bothered with, I was asked to draft the contract. Since we had done the underlying work previously and the project was an application based on that platform, in the contract I retained all the IP and gave the client usage rights.

As it turned out, the system we then delivered became core to the company's functioning, and they wanted to outright "own" the platform. I resisted and was promptly invited to meet with the top lawyer along with the executive in charge.

Since the meeting was happening in New York, the lawyer was wearing a fancy suit and a starched shirt with his initials in gold on the sleeves. From the get-go, that lawyer began growling at me, making sure I understood how important he was. He immediately got to the point. "Dr. Sahin, I am puzzled. We paid for it, and we own it. Do you not understand?"

He was actually tapping his watch to let me know how precious his time was, how it shouldn't even be wasted on such an obvious matter.

I responded that I liked his shirt.

Surprised and then quickly indignant, he declared this was a very serious conversation indeed.

I agreed with him, and since I liked his shirt, I wanted to know if he paid for it.

Of course he'd paid for it, he insisted. Why was I asking such silly questions?

I then asked him if I could buy the pattern.

He grew more upset.

I said that since he paid for that shirt, and further since he was claiming that when you pay for something you own the IP, then surely he must own the shirt's IP. I let that sit, then delivered the punch line.

Since he was a lawyer, he surely knew that *rights* are as described and agreed to by contract. My contract clearly stated that my company owned the IP and his company had usage rights. If his company wanted to own the platform IP, I would be happy to sell at the right price. But why would they be interested, I wondered aloud, since they already had full usage rights?

The lawyer was dumbfounded.

The executive then graciously agreed with me and said he had no interest in obtaining the platform. What would he do with it, anyway?

I can still remember the anger shooting out of the lawyer's eyes at me, and at the executive, as well.

I would tell this same fancy-shirt story many times over the years and usually win. But not always. To achieve an overall winning record, I had to lay other supportive arguments on the table.

Are they really paying or just financing?

Once, a big-company lawyer completely refused to budge off the IP ownership issue. His company was paying for it, they owned it, end of discussion. What to do?

I pointed out that they were, in fact, financing this project, not paying for it. Yes, financing it because there were all kinds of contingencies built in. Things like milestone payments, change-order decisions, etc. And all these contingencies had strings attached to the payments we would receive along the way.

My company was bearing all the ongoing risks, and they were financing it as we went from one milestone to the other. We could just as well go to a bank and get a loan, and it would have fewer caveats. So, instead of their "financing" the project, we would finance it ourselves through to the project's end. Then they could decide if they wanted to buy the deliverables outright—like a purchase transaction.

In taking that approach, however, they would rightly have no say in the development as we went along. Why not instead finance the project, participate in its progress, and at the end get the rights that really mattered—specifically, the usage rights?

He was initially confused but then saw the logic and backed off from his "we are paying for it; so, we will own it" position.

At the project's end, they got only the usage rights, and we got to keep the IP, both the preexisting bundle and the newly developed one during the project.

When Is Owning IP Not Worth It?

Another approach is to point out the inherent costs/risks of IP ownership. Should a third party want to (a) commission a project based on the original IP, (b) ask for customization of the existing platform, or (c) develop any derivative products ... then their ownership of any resultant IP would also mean they are responsible for any infringements.

Indeed, if another entity infringed or outright stole the IP, the owner of the IP would then have to sue or at least enter into a cross-licensing arrangement—both of which could incur indeterminate costs.

There would also be the cost associated with licensing the under-lying IP derivatives, for which a higher price would be expected.

When I've pointed out these underlying costs and liabilities to many a lawyer and their bosses, they often become suddenly keen on exploring alternative ways to reach their principal objectives.

While executives may be reluctant to say why they want to own the IP, it is useful to help tease the reasons out. Why do they really want it?

Usually, the answer is to keep their competitors at bay and maintain an advantage. It's almost an instinctual drive in the C-suite. When you know the true objectives, it becomes much easier to marshal counterarguments. Here's one argument worth making:

Once a commissioned project becomes a key component in the client's product portfolio, it will result in a new array of favorable outcomes (e.g., faster response times, lower latency, smoother customer interactions). And those outcomes will be able to be marketed and properly priced along with the rest of the company's portfolio. Having these benefits will be the real barrier to competition, more so than the ownership of the IP.

Further to that and building the argument stronger, no real competitor will be sitting on their hands. Sooner or later, they'll develop or adapt similar products to attain the same outcomes—especially if valued in the marketplace. And while they are striving to catch up, the client will be looking to secure the next advantage and at a lower cost if their lawyer's IP ownership push is resisted.

This law of business survival is ultimately the strongest argument.

It's also common for a client to request *exclusive rights* to the IP. This is a loser as well.

Exclusivity is in effect a sale but at a lower price with all the risks of ownership remaining with the IP developer. To deal with this, it's good to point out that exclusivity is a de facto sale. Therefore, the license price should be a multiple of the nonexclusive license. This explanation injects some business reality into things. As well, you can talk about diluted forms of exclusivity such as excluding licenses to a set of named competitors of the client, geographic exclusivity, and selected features exclusivity.

Contracts are the reinforcing structure of the startup's house. It's nonoptional to pay attention to them if the Lean Startup hopes to transform into a Lean Company and then enjoy a Rich Exit. Especially the exit.

You might view contracts as complex and as such the domain of lawyers and leave the drafting and the negotiations in their hands.

Understandable, but often not a good approach.

The key clauses of contracts are inarguably the purview of management and must be understood. But only the key clauses, not the minutiae.

And the key clauses are not as complicated as their reputation suggests. A standard business contract can stretch for pages, but only the key clauses deserve your fullest attention:

- IP ownership
- Definition of damages
- Limitation of liability
- Representations and warranties
- Indemnification
- Definition of satisfactory work
- Payment terms
- Duration of the contract
- Assignability of the contract
- Cancellation terms and clauses
- Confidentiality
- Nonsolicitation

There will be additional clauses that become important in specialty cases. However, focusing on these key clauses is essential—especially as negotiations begin and trade-off decisions are required to seal the contract to both sides' satisfaction. With contracts in order, a Lean Startup can move on to the fun part—transitioning into a Lean Company.

CHAPTER 1

TAKEAWAY PRINCIPLES AND VOCABULARY

- Identify an initial portfolio of offers.

- Couple your offers with rough price ranges.

- Learn the art of doing more with less.

- Begin developing a vocabulary around your offers.

- Seed relevant communities with increasingly refined offers.

- Launch the first of many noisy explorations for docking sites for your offers.

- Build the right contacts by drawing a circle around the cross.

- Radiate beyond cross-and-circle contacts for new opportunities.

- Recognize contracts as the load-bearing walls of your Lean Startup.

2

BECOMING A
LEAN COMPANY

Note: Going forward, as appropriate, I will designate LS *for Lean Startup,* LC *for Lean Company, and* RE *for Rich Exit.*

In this short chapter, I will discuss a fundamental pillar of the organization—people. This involves the sourcing of candidates, extending offers and hiring, and devising compensation plans. After all, a company is a company of people.

Some entrepreneurs either want to or are able to take the diamond lane by tapping funding sources and hiring a C-suite team of executives right away. Since we're focusing on remaining as lean as possible at each step, there are principles to guide us.

We've discussed the critical importance of the founder's firm grasp on the basics of contracts—no matter how well funded or supported. It's also important at the early stages of a company, when many front-office tasks are not that complex, for the founder to be a jack-of-all-trades, knowing how to handle the accounting and finance—including payroll, billing, receivables and payables, cash management, banking, and taxes; procurement of supplies and capital equipment; handling basic legal matters; operations (particularly any leases entered into); and, foremost, HR, specifically hiring.

Then in the next chapter, we'll get into the company's structural functions, including offices, leasing, HR, legal, accounting, and the like.

At the outset, an LS is like an efficiency apartment unit: all in one. An LC is more like a house with many rooms for different purposes. A bigger LC is more like an apartment complex, a mall, or a skyscraper—or a portfolio of them.

When you have only a couple of contracts and invoices on the company letterhead, all these structural functions are straightforward. But count on the complexities to start piling up when you have double-digit counts of employees, contracts, clients, and projects. When that stage is reached, then hiring the right staff to handle all these tasks becomes much easier—because you've taken the time to understand the basics of running a company and you know what to ask in interviews.

Hiring

Legally a one-person entity is a company that I euphemistically describe as "you, you, and you." But in a true sense, a company becomes real when you have company—that is, people. There are many ways of making those first hires.

The typical approach is to develop a job description and list the qualifications that a "successful" candidate is to have and then post it to the various boards. Often the list of qualifications includes having experience in the relevant area, such as "accounting" if that's the position being hired for. This is the typical way, right?

I suggest a different way, what I call AAWE: high aptitude first, then positive and team-oriented attitude, then willingness to learn and be taught, and finally the extra, experience.

In my travels abroad, I've seen the educational systems of every major country. I've seen how US excellence owes a lot to its well-developed structures that are optimized for teaching and learning, along with an emphasis on validation and feedback through a robust process of quizzes, graded homework, graded classroom participation, exams, term papers, field reports, theses, etc. No student in the United States, no matter how advanced, can escape this rigorous process.

And at all major colleges, the teachers also get validated by being required to publish. These days students can also validate teachers, or at least their teaching, through online evaluations.

I sought to build this process of validation and feedback into the organizational architecture of my own startup from the outset. I had been inspired by the academic ecosystem and wanted to port it into the business world in a meaningful and appropriate way—to make it an everyday practice. In that sense, I was hoping to strike a balance between over- and underreliance on the scientific method. I knew it was easier said than done.

So, I sought to create a recruiting and hiring formula that would break with so many of the practices of the time—which I viewed as flawed.

I aimed for a formula that would take our company's name and story into the finest schools nationwide, help us beat out the top recruiting companies in finding talent despite being a name few had yet heard of, and ensure that the talent truly represented a good cultural fit for the organization we were engineering.

For me as an academic stepping into the business world, the classical industrial hiring model I saw everyone using struck me as stale as last week's bread. Possibly because it was designed decades before the word *knowledge* had ever been put in front of *workers*.

For starters, the model began with de-risking. Applicants had to arrive with years of prior experience, subject-matter expertise, or both. Yet in academia, I'd found that students with high aptitudes but no prior experience could come up to speed on a subject very quickly and then continue progressing. A complex undergraduate degree is completed in just four years with a working mastery of many subjects achieved. After two years, a student with any undergraduate background becomes a "master" of business administration, no less.

Such quick pickup is rarely the case, however, in the "real world" with experienced or de-risked individuals. They tend to be set in their ways and thus slower to adapt to new organizational structures. Things have to run their way, or else they are thrown off their game. After all, they are being hired for just that—*their way.*

I wanted to go another way.

I didn't want to start out facing a wall of resistance to the academic principles I meant to test (such as, as we'll see, teach and learn, learn and teach, noisy explorations, ambiguity tolerance, situational leadership, and dynamic configurability). I wanted to see if the principles would work. Hiring green, part-time students at first gave me an excellent canvas for testing these principles—because the students didn't come in with preconceived notions.

I knew the students were top talents since I had taught them at MIT. And right away, they began proving themselves exceptional in their work product. They also resonated with the principles in an almost uncanny way. I found this interplay encouraging, to say the least. So, I next sought to backfill my understanding of what made these students such exceptional members of our team. It took a while, but I finally narrowed it down to four key attributes:

1. They had a high aptitude and could pick up new things quickly.

2. They had a great attitude with high energy, passion, and an eagerness to go the extra mile, do whatever was required, and work with a team.

3. They had a willingness to learn and be coached.

4. They had something extra, which was often their experience (and I found this to be the least important of the four).

With this assessment, a future hiring principle emerged: high aptitude first, then positive and team-oriented attitude, then willingness to learn and be taught, and finally, an extra, usually experience. We nicknamed it AAWE.

Finding Candidates

To be sure, when finding (often called "sourcing") quality new hires, recruiters are a great expedient. However, there are other avenues that can be just as effective, if not more so, and much less costly.

When you use the AAWE approach, every new college graduate becomes a viable candidate. Almost every university posts résumé books. It can be fun (or at least I found it so) to flip through these books and identify great candidates. Universities also have alumni lists—another great resource. Then there are all the commercial resources such as LinkedIn and display ads on online boards.

Making direct personal contact with potential hires in an age of email and text communications is not that hard. Even if the hit rate is low, if the funnel is kept wide open, there can be more than enough candidates coming through.

In posting for candidates, keep the focus on the intangibles rather than long lists of qualifications. For instance, why not share that "We cherish excellence and aim for impact. Our company is where you can grow because we emphasize learning and teaching. We are all accessible to each other." This is meaningful information—more so for today's Millennial and Gen Z audiences than ever before.

At the outset and assuming the company structure is still mostly you, you, and you, there is no choice but for you to do the interviewing. It's never easy to carve out enough time to do it right. The temptation becomes to prescreen the candidates, basically to put them through trials and tribulations. But don't; just don't.

Take the time—because your hires matter more than anything. You recruit the best candidates by ably describing all the goodness inherent in your company, from the people through the visions to the impact you're aiming to make, and nobody can communicate that better than you.

Once an individual shows enough interest in your organization, then you can gently go about exploring the "fit." In doing this, be sure to emphasize right up front that the candidate is obviously qualified, as otherwise she would not have been invited for the interview, and if the company were not attractive, she would not have come. So, the mission is to determine the fit, pure and simple.

If you see the value in practicing AAWE, where the second *A* stands for "positive attitude and collaboration," then why not make the interview a positive and collaborative one? It just makes sense, right?

It makes sense again when it comes to writing ding letters because you can honestly say, "You are qualified, but we found a better match. We'll keep your CV in our files should things change."

After the first several successful hires, who should then take over candidate sourcing and interviewing?

Still you … even if the company is fast growing. And now it can strain the old schedule. But the benefits to the company in your continuing to lead the recruiting and interviewing process are many. Nobody is going to articulate the company's vision as compellingly as you. Having a firsthand link to any new hires will help you socialize them with the team—speeding their acceptance and their coming up to speed.

An LS works best when everyone on the staff is tightly networked, like a family—yes, just like a family. Being involved in the recruiting process from alpha (recruiting) to omicron (onboarding) to omega (intranetworking) gives you that familial connection to every person in the company.

There is another reason to be intimately involved in this process—one that is often overlooked.

Fair to say, I learned at an early age to cherish excellence and believe in something I would later identify as a meritocracy. I saw it firsthand in the MIT ecosystem. Theirs was a talent to delight in, to emulate. So, as I entered the private sector, I was saddened that a merit-based mindset was not universally held.

Some people with exemplary skill sets of their own want desperately to be viewed as standouts in their domains, so they will surround themselves with the mediocre and the lackadaisical to accomplish their aims. It's a form of insecurity, surely. But whatever it is, it eats away at the very foundation of a knowledge organization. With this thought, another principle:

Excellence does not always surround itself with excellence, but must.

Later, I was to learn from a dean at MIT of a complementary insight. When I asked how MIT manages to remain excellent, he said by getting rid of the "good" as quickly as possible. Since the enemy of the excellent is the good, then it stands to reason that the good will be constantly working to hang on to their positions, which will frustrate or intimidate or, even worse, agitate the excellent, who will then leave. In due time, the institution will be just … good.

If you relinquish your role as the first stop in the recruiting/ interviewing process, the additional hires might be just good and, in time, push out the core of excellent people. Much better to act as the internal recruiter shepherding exceptional candidates through their interviews with other principals in the organization. While this takes no small time commitment, it's only a fraction of the time required to undo the damage a "good" hire can cause.

How many of the staff should be involved in these candidate interviews?

There are many reasons, some of them surprising, for strictly limiting the number of staffers who meet with a candidate. This is because, invariably, someone on the team takes it upon themselves to educate the candidate about the company's internal workings and projects. But then if the candidate doesn't join on, all that deep knowledge can find its way into the hands of direct competitors. Not so good.

I've heard many startup founders admit that as their organizations grew, they wanted to continue as lead interviewer, but time constraints made it difficult. It's a valid concern. But coupled with that old yarn "If you don't have time to do it right, when will you have time to do it over?" is this one: "If you don't have time to find an excellent team, how will your team ever be excellent?"

Candidate Selection—Best versus Excellent

Search firms and engines all claim to be able to source the best talent. That's their marketing department talking, of course. However, be aware that the best of the good candidates is still just good. Worse, the best of the bad candidates is just bad.

Also, what happens when excellence is found but the recruiting continues on anyway? Very likely, the excellent will take another offer. So, finding the "best" might well end up with the good, not the excellent. Better to stop the search process when there is an excellent candidate and make the offer.

Compensation

Once a candidate is identified, next comes the make-or-break process: the offer, in particular the compensation package. What to include and how to present it?

My recommendation is to describe the intangibles in the offer letter first. All that is very much part of compensation. If salary were the only driver, why would people become professors with all the work required to obtain a PhD, knowing that they'll make less than their private sector counterparts? Same for highly educated writers or healthcare workers who cherish the intangibles of work in those fields.

With the salary discussion comes the usually troublesome stock options—the so-called "piece of the action." On this, I'll get personal. Across the decades, I have seen excellent minds join early-stage companies on the lure of stock options and then, for a multitude of reasons, move on and see their options expiring. Then those who join the company later end up enjoying the benefits of a successful company, because success often takes time.

All this assumes the company does succeed. That is why when I hired many hundreds of top technologists into Kenan Systems, I always told them the odds of success right from the start. It was good for me to keep in mind, and the same was true for candidates who might be swayed by the options—however uncertain they might be financially.

So, in addition to telling candidates that stock options are iffy gambles on an uncertain future, I told them that Kenan Systems did not offer stock options but instead paid salaries substantially above market. If the candidate was interviewing at more than one company and had a competing offer that included stock options, that usually meant the salary offer was below market. The candidate was essentially paying for the options and indirectly financing the company making the offer, often a small, risky company.

It is risky to join a startup or a small company to begin with. Why take two risks on the same company? Why not take the above-market salary offer, and invest the extra cash in a solid portfolio? Over time, that portfolio can outperform all but the luckiest few of stock options holders.

Compensation Afterward: Profit Sharing versus Gainsharing

It should be a matter of corporate policy that all employees share in the financial success of the company in some meaningful way. But there are better ways than stock options, which have the distorting effect of lending the holder "ownership" rights.

One alternative is profit sharing. Yet with many companies, there will be a long wait time until profitability is reached and any profits shared—making the concept less than enticing, even demotivational.

At Kenan Systems, I used and continue to recommend gainsharing. With this, any cash distributions to the team are based on the overall performance of the company and then an individual team member's contribution.

For the first part of the equation, you have a suite of metrics that include total revenue, customer satisfaction, on-time and on-budget delivery, and core value attainment. Some are quantifiable metrics, clearly, and some qualitative. Taken together, they represent an overall report card to be used in determining how much cash should be distributed. Then you determine each employee's gain share based on their performance reviews—from a satisfactory evaluation to very good to outstanding, etc. This rating should be applied only to the workload they can influence or contribute to—a distinction that can be readily understood.

By contrast, profit sharing can be an opaque metric involving a myriad of accounting measures such as depreciation, last-in, inventory methods, pricing, discounts, tax, etc. In not using this approach, you avoid the discomfort of having to answer difficult questions from employees about how their cash package was devised, answers that are sure to upset as many as they please.

This twin approach of paying above market and using gainsharing with periodic cash distributions proved to enhance staff retention, as well, in my experience.

CHAPTER 2

TAKEAWAY PRINCIPLES AND VOCABULARY

- ⇒ Hire using AAWE: high aptitude first, then positive and team-oriented attitude, then willingness to learn and be taught, finally an extra, such as experience.
- ⇒ Recruit talent first, then assess for fit.
- ⇒ Excellence does not always surround itself with excellence, but must.
- ⇒ The good pushes out the excellent, so banish the good ASAP.
- ⇒ Consider using gainsharing over profit sharing to reward employees.

3

BUILDING AND POPULATING THE STRUCTURES

We're picking up with an LS that is becoming an LC and ready to move out of the basement or whatever the tight quarters have been. At this point, there is a stable set of customers responding to a portfolio of offers. There is a team coming together and a differentiated structure. It's clear to all, however, that this structure needs both more people and more space (though space is an evolving notion postpandemic).

Premises

I bring up the company's selection of office space early on because, in so many ways, it can shape the character and operations of an LS evolving into an LC. Where to move, how to move, how much space, lease terms, who goes where—a lot of questions come up.

Chances are that the current space evolved ad hoc, is overly tight and cramping everyone's style, and a move to better quarters is still warranted even though the company aims to continue running lean. Chances are also that optimism is high that the company will be growing rapidly.

That said, moves are disruptive time sinks, and no fun at all. So, the question is this: Should the company lease space that accommodates the anticipated near-term needs and the potential long-term expansion plans as well? It's tempting to lease twenty thousand square feet when the short-term need might be only ten thousand square feet, for example.

My own inclination is to lease just enough space for the short term, negotiating possible options for both renewal and additional space. I've seen too many companies take on extra "expansion space" on long-term leases and then feel dwarfed by so much empty space when growth dipped unexpectedly. Better to run out of space than to be staring at empty halls as well as to have a liability on the balance sheet.

The Lease

I strongly recommend that CEOs get heavily involved in lease negotiations. Most of it is boilerplate, anyway, with only a handful of clauses that require focused attention. A few hours invested in this paperwork at the outset can save huge sums later on and keep the company running lean.

Lease costs are typically expressed in dollars per square foot per year. But is it the net space or gross space? If gross, what is included? Corridors, elevators, utility rooms? You want to know. The rent per square foot might be reasonable, but the total rent might not be if it includes everything down to the kitchen sink. Also important is how square footage is computed. Is it from inside wall to inside wall? Some landlords craftily use outside walls in their measurements.

Is the rent gross (meaning utilities, taxes, maintenance, etc.) or triple net (meaning a prorated share of all extras will be added to the base rent by a formula of the landlord's choosing)? It makes sense to learn that formula and also ask to see charges from prior years as a reference point. Then, an annual inflation adjustment is usually built in.

Rarely is the space in move-in condition. Whatever the condition, there is typically an allowance made to fit the incoming tenant's needs with a certain amount offered for tenant improvements. You want to take full advantage of these improvements, of course, but recognize that in later years when the rent increases, these improvements will effectively increase the base rent increase—as the landlord is amortizing them over the life of the lease. Good to find out the amortization time frame. You don't want to pay for core improvements that will benefit the next tenant.

The life of the lease is also important to understand. Landlords often want five- or seven- or even ten-year periods. For a small company, a three-year period is ideal with options to renew—preferably yearly for two or three years. It is good to determine the renewal rent amount, as well.

Also look at taking an option on adjoining space. That can be a good buffer solution and much better than leasing a lot of extra space, just in case. I've seen companies that occupy a small space (five thousand square feet) take an option to lease a multiple of that space for anticipated growth.

What if instead of growth there is shrinkage, hopefully temporarily? Can the extra space be sublet? Depends on the lease. It's a good idea to get permission to sublet as part of the lease terms.

Two more matters. First, who is responsible for maintenance? If the tenant is, that could be a cost and time burden. Best to have the landlord take charge, except for small items. Second, when the lease is over, what happens to the premises? Broom clean or restoration to the original conditions? And if it becomes necessary to stay beyond the lease's end, say a month or two, it's good to have a provision for that in the lease contract. Even if it means the rent goes up significantly, it's a safety valve.

These are the main issues. Thus informed, the CEO can effectively enter into lease negotiations. A dollar saved is a dollar earned, and good negotiations can save a lot of dollars. Landlords tend to be seasoned negotiators and are very much swayed by the leverage you may have in choosing their location over another. So, come to the table showing neither enthusiasm nor desperation. Have alternative locations lined up, and let the landlord know you do when you begin negotiating.

As an aside, your participation in lease negotiations is good practice for negotiating contracts with prospective clients. The dynamics are similar. Why not sharpen your skills rather than leave it to the office manager or operations lead?

Office Layout

Just like most mammals, we humans are territorial. From who goes where in the office layout to how much space is surrounding the desk to who sits at nearby desks … these questions can trigger our most primal instincts leading to emotional outbursts that upset what otherwise should be a happy time—the company is bursting at the seams!

So, there's a need in these situations for move tolerance. The move is going to bring up all kinds of emotions, including long-sublimated ones. If there is a path across this emotional battlefield, it has to hew to business objectives first, before devolving into concerns about rank in the company, size of the windows or the view, proximity to the bathrooms, etc.

These days, cubicles are part of office life. Why not start with everyone in cubicles except those who require privacy, such as the in-house lawyer? Let the conference rooms serve their purpose of holding meetings and giving the team a place to go for an uninterrupted or personal call.

What if you are moving into already finished offices? Use those offices with doors as conference rooms; rehab them if necessary for sizing. If there are more offices than needed, assign them to individuals who most need them for business reasons. If these offices are large enough, put two people in them so the feeling of exclusivity goes away.

I've tried all these approaches, and when an office layout was decided based on clear business objectives, they worked.

Nonetheless, back at Kenan Systems, I could not convince my board chairman, Howard Johnson (then simultaneously the chair of the MIT board and, prior to that, MIT president), that I was right about all this. He insisted that the CEO of a company like ours was the key strategic salesperson as well as the key client relationship manager and that clients would not think highly of me sitting in a cubicle next to the coffee machine.

So, I took a window office, a large one, with the caveat that it would also be a conference room. My office became the desk in the corner, and the large table at the other end became the conference room. Since a lot of the time when I was in the office, I had meetings, it all worked well, or at least until one point in our growth.

One day upon returning from a trip, I saw a sign on the door of my dual-use office: *Meeting in Progress.* The staff had taken me seriously, and there was a meeting going on. So, I dropped my bag by the door and started walking around interacting with colleagues spontaneously. To this day, when I arrive at work, I don't immediately aim for my office but roam the corridors, interrupting and being interrupted. It's not unusual for an hour to pass before I finally arrive in my office.

Another touchy situation relates here. I was hiring a lawyer who had previously worked at a big company in a big private office, and that's what he expected at Kenan Systems as well. We came to terms on all matters, and he accepted our offer. To preempt any issues prior to his beginning work, I explained our policy that window offices were shared and if single offices were needed, they would be interior ones. He said he really wanted "an office with a window." I said I would think about it.

When he arrived, I led him to an interior office and could see his face turning red. Expecting as much, I said, "This was what you wanted, an office with a window." He was puzzled until I pointed out the framed glass window we had leaned against the wall. "As a lawyer, you should be satisfied since our informal contract was for an office with a window, and that is what you got." He let out a laugh but felt compelled to go along as he really liked the place and the job.

Communication Networks

A lot of planned work gets done in offices and in meetings with agendas. A lot of creative work happens in chance encounters and random conversations. This is well known, and it's why I've highlighted two relevant principles: noisy exploration and interruptibility.

Who sits where in an office can significantly impact the kinds of conversations people have. Nearest office neighbors tend to interact a lot. Research confirms the obvious—interactions drop off steeply as the distance between two offices increases.

When I was at Bell Labs, I was struck by the layout with the bathrooms at either end of long, long corridors. I was told that it was by design. It forced the staff to walk by many, many offices, and even if they did not or could not interact on the way (Need to go!), perhaps on the way back, they might. I suspected that office design contributed in some degree to Bell Labs' legendary innovation output.

I also saw the byproduct of an office's seating chart back in my academic days. I was a visiting professor at Harvard University. I was given an office the permanent staff didn't want: a small one directly opposite the elevators. The previous occupant of this office had placed his desk with his back facing the elevators, for privacy.

I did the opposite. I faced the elevators, and whoever came out had no choice but to make eye contact with me and get a nod and smile. Some would curiously venture in, to find out who I was. Soon I got to know almost everybody and enjoyed many noisy explorations. By the end of the year, I was in collaboration with at least a dozen of the faculty. It was my most productive academic year, thanks to my taking the office nobody wanted.

At this point in our LS's journey, there is space to grow, staff situated where they can be their most productive selves, work orders coming in, deliverables going out, and invoices blossoming into cash. It's time now to structure the support functions more formally.

Human Resources (HR)

Earlier, I recommended that the CEO try to become a sweeping generalist, initially handling as many of the support functions (HR, accounting, contracting and legal, billing, banking, and even payroll) as possible. This not only gives you a basic feel for every critical piece of the company; it helps instill the kind of culture you desire at each level of the company. But when an organization gets to a certain size, this heavy participation in support functions becomes counterproductive, even untenable.

This becomes the time to build out the support functions and do it in a manner that keeps the company culture inviolate and precludes these functions from naturally expanding beyond the core benefits they convey. For as with other pieces of the organization, the support functions can fast become self-empowered islands of their own. In fact, they can get there faster, owing to the more siloed nature of their work.

A generalist CEO who by now has a good working knowledge of these support functions can easily spot a fast-growing power concentration and avert it early on—while still possible and without too great a disruption.

This is yet another argument for the CEO to remain involved in hiring at the support unit level, to be sure those hired into these positions are in alignment with the company's organizational dynamic.

We've discussed the power of AAWE as a hiring model. I recommend using this model to build up the support groups for the growing organization. And when possible, try to hire *functions* over *managers*. Let me explain, using HR as an example.

Among the key functions of HR are benefits administration (health insurance, mostly), compliance with a plethora of regulations, and hiring team members. The classical route is to hire the HR manager and let him or her populate the organization. Certainly an expedient and reasonable approach.

But my recommendation for hiring an HR manager is to begin the process looking for an AAWE candidate who has entry-level experience in the three HR functions mentioned above, or a combination of them. For instance, a benefits coordinator who can also do compliance. For a small company, this should be doable. For sourcing candidates, an entry-level person can roam the corridors of colleges and use alumni databases and LinkedIn to find handfuls of good candidates.

With an entry-level hire, you can coach them in your vision. Being relatively inexperienced, they're more likely to adapt to the company's culture and modus operandi. Starting with an experienced

HR manager/executive, on the other hand, means they'll be importing whatever culture and practices they've learned over the years. This can be useful, since these experiences can be valuable, but it can also spread like kudzu that overgrows the culture you're aiming for.

In this HR position—which is fully a support position, remember—it is usually better to have someone dedicated to executing your company vision rather than importing somebody else's.

The approach I recommend is consistent with remaining lean: it is evolution over disruption, and it helps to preempt downstream power concentration in HR. In many companies, HR is not only a force but one people try to avoid because it is seen as a gate to be hurdled or folderol to be avoided. This is partially unfair, but nonetheless true—all the more so because when HR becomes a full-fledged department, it should remain disempowered so that it can be more effective.

There are certainly pros and cons to this disempowered approach to HR, and talented people can disagree with my approach to it—especially in certain contexts and circumstances.

In the context of an LS becoming an LC, I have found that a strong-willed HR director will take over hiring and compensation management, as well.

In hiring, the empowered HR usually follows the classical model. A position needs filling, so a job description is written up articulating the background and skills required, an advertisement is posted, applicants are screened, initial interviews are conducted, and finalists are produced.

For a mature enterprise, this classical hiring model has its merits. However, it is inconsistent with the AAWE approach I favor—especially for an LS evolving into an LC.

I know many will disagree with this approach here. I've heard it said many times over the years that this AAWE approach, coupled as it is with a disempowered HR office, is fully unorthodox and even suspect. I can respond only with my own experience in hiring thousands of people into a full range of corporate positions, along with the feedback received from Kenan Systems staff who, after leaving our company, went on to practice AAWE and disempowered HR in the companies they led.

So, bear in mind that these recommendations should always be applied only in a supportive context. Also note that it is much easier to go from AAWE and disempowered HR to the classical hiring model than the other way around. Once the empowered HR becomes the department to avoid, it's hard to reset the employees' mindsets.

At Kenan Systems, we applied this approach with a young and talented HR team, each handling a different aspect of HR. After a while, this junior team found itself bursting at the seams, and we needed to hire a senior person to run the HR group. I turned to my AAWE approach, as I almost always tried to. The finalist had tons of experience, which seemed okay because she scored high on the A and A and W. She really liked the company and expressed a keen interest in joining. Okay.

I then explained that as head of HR, she would be disempowered. She was instantly puzzled and, I could see, took that to suggest a lack of trust in her. She had gone to top schools known for their first-rate HR programs and had most recently left an executive HR position at a world-class company for personal reasons. So, after all that, she would now be stepping down. Hmm.

I continued to *describe* what I meant by disempowered and did not *define* it, and I could sense an internal frown turning up, an intrigue growing. She could see that the staff she would be coordinating, though not supervising, were in fact really talented individuals.

Time passed. She not only came to understand the value of disempowerment but became a fan of it. She discovered that HR had become truly supportive of an overall higher level of employee achievement. In that sense, actually, more empowered.

I also talked with our new HR lead about situational leadership and checks and balances, and in due time she switched over from her old big-company thinking to be one of our most ardent advocates of these LS to LC principles. In time, she worked closely with me to develop additional HR principles:

- Hire from within with repurposing.
- In lean management, hire up from the bottom.
- In performance reviews, use the GRRITS framework (focusing on an employee's goals, responsibilities, requests, interests, talents, and skills), and we'll talk more about this later.
- Amplify and propagate the strengths and innovations of the staff being reviewed and put the burden of dealing with weaknesses on the staff.
- Mix cultural training, content training, and cross-training.
- Staff departures mean opportunities for replacements from within and reconfiguring the roles.
- Never try to clone staff members who have left but evolve the role they had.

Accounting

I recommend AAWE for building the accounting team, as well. The initial hire is a bookkeeper, then an outside firm for heavy-duty accounting functions and tax filings, and then a junior accountant. Whenever possible, promote up from the existing team.

In the first company I founded, for the first four years, I handled all accounting functions: keeping the books, computing billing rates, submitting invoices, doing the banking, etc. When we hit ten employees, I turned payroll over to a service bureau. Once the board was formed, by which time we were pushing a headcount of twenty-five, I engaged a major accounting firm primarily for the audit function.

I simultaneously hired an E (Experience) accountant/controller, only to regret it. He had his ways, and that was that. And he was always behind schedule. Fortunately, I had also hired the junior accountant. To my relief, when the experienced controller left for greener pastures, the junior took over, and alongside the outside firm, we managed well until the company was well past a head count of fifty.

When looking for accounting talent, keep in mind that major accounting firms hire new graduates right out of school and, after three years, winnow them. In the meantime, those hires get excellent experience. It is a great pool to reach into and hire.

Staffing up accounting is important, but even more important is shaping the operations of accounting so that it is a true support function. Much like with HR and legal, if left alone they tend toward empowered moves and can quickly become more of an obstacle than an enabler. The longer they are left alone, the more complex the unwinding process becomes. Hence my earlier suggestion that from the outset, you get a general grounding in accounting and even practice it some.

As also with HR and legal, accounting can appear complex at first—but most of that complexity relates to rules, regulations, and GAAP (generally accepted accounting principles). The basics of debits and credits are truly straightforward, and a CEO must have a working understanding of these.

There are three fundamental financial statements to fully understand.

1. BALANCE SHEET (B/S)

On the left side of the balance sheet go the values of the company's assets (cash, receivables, and cash equivalents, such as securities, fixed assets like buildings or equipment, inventory, and intangible assets like patents—all using historical cost minus adjustments like depreciation, amortization, and allowance for receivables that might not be received). On the right side of the balance sheets go claims against those assets, which are the liabilities and the claims of shareholders. Any unusual matters are handled in footnotes.

2. THE INCOME STATEMENT (I/S)

Where the B/S shows a snapshot of the company's finances, the I/S shows the flow or change over time. Think of the B/S as the water in a tank and the I/S as the inflows and outflows over periods such as a month, quarter, or year.

The IS starts with gross revenues, known as the top line. Gross revenues do not take into account any expenses or adjustments incurred to generate those revenues but are a clean statement of net operating income for the period.

Operating expenses are the costs incurred to produce the revenue. The biggest is typically the cost of goods sold (COGS). Payroll costs can run higher if it is a services company. Then there are supplies, other consumables, marketing, advertising, etc. Somewhat confusing expenses are depreciation and amortization, and they require some study. Even more confusing is "goodwill," which is amortized according to IRS rules.

If an incurred cost is not related to generating revenue, then it is a deduction to net income with a footnote explaining what and why. For instance, if a piece of equipment is scrapped but still has book value, the equipment is written off and the residual net book value (original price minus accumulated depreciation) is deducted from the bottom line as a loss on disposal or sale of assets.

Spend a few hours learning basic accounting, and it quickly becomes clear that there is an enormous amount of fungibility in what can be, or should be, rather cut and dried. It is good to know the more arbitrary matters so that decisions are not warped and distorted.

A simple example of this is the depreciation of fixed assets. What is the life, and what is the rate? No hard and fast rules. If an asset is purchased at $100,000 and the economic life is assumed to be ten years, using linear depreciation, each year's income will be hit with a $10,000 depreciation expense. What if it is accelerated at a 20 percent rate? First-year expense would be $20,000, then 20 percent of the remaining $80,000, which is $16,000 and so on. Very different depreciation expense profiles.

Now along comes Congress with legislation meant to stimulate the economy by reducing corporate taxes through accelerated depreciation rules. For instance, in the year of purchase, that $100,000 equipment could be fully written off, lowering taxable income. Great for the company, but misleading to managers and investors. What to do?

No choice but to have multiple accounts for the same item such as a piece of equipment or even a building. Is that multiple sets of books, one for the government and one for GAAP? One could say so, but then having multiple sets of books comes across as fraud when, in fact, it is required.

Here is another example. Tax payments could be on so-called accrual or GAAP accounting or on a cash basis, which is typically used by smaller companies, especially if they are LLCs. Once again, the tax books would be different than the GAAP books. However, for GAAP purposes, the tax books have to be reconciled with the stewardship financials. The handling of this can get tricky. Be that as it may, understanding the differences can allow you to materially impact the bottom line. It is simply a matter of knowing what is allowed and what is not. (As a side note, it only becomes fraud when items are *kept off the books*.)

Here is where one of my own guiding principles, that of ambiguity tolerance, comes into play. For I can assert with great certainty that there is no such thing as certainty when it comes to income. There's no certain income when it comes to accounting for it. So much depends on the underlying assumptions that are used to account for that income.

A far bigger source of variability is cash accounting versus accrual accounting. GAAP typically requires accrual. Cash basis is often used in small companies for tax purposes, but the IRS has to consent to it. One cannot go back and forth. Best to know the rules.

In the cash world, revenue is recognized when cash comes in, and it's the same for expenses, with several major exceptions. Example: A big sale is made on an installment plan. With accrual, the whole amount is recognized as revenue, and the part that will be realized in the future goes into receivables on the left side of the B/S as a short-term asset.

In cash accounting, revenue is recognized when payments are received, and expenses are recognized when cash is paid out. A major exception, among others, is depreciation.

3. CASH FLOW (C/F) OR SOURCES AND USES

Here, we see where cash comes from, e.g., sales, loans, deposits, investors, and tax refunds. And we see where cash goes, e.g., operations, capital purchases.

With such cursory knowledge, you are not going to pass an accounting exam, but you can get involved in the accounting function and ensure that it is linked to the decision-making process and does not warp that process.

Another example: A restaurant is visited by its accountant. As he enters the premises, he spots a vending machine in the corner and asks the restaurant owner what it's all about. The owner, with pride, says, "A salesperson came in telling me that if I allowed that vending machine to be installed, I would not need to pay anything except for electricity, and I would get five cents on each item vended. Of course, I enthusiastically agreed. What a nice way to make money without any investment and also please my customers."

The accountant is puzzled and wonders if the owner has really made a wise decision. Why, in his view?

Well, the accountant thinks, the owner just doesn't understand how costing is done. He proceeds to educate the owner. "Did you consider allocating to that machine part of the rent and utilities since it is clearly taking up space? Did you factor in overhead like maintenance, security, cleaning, and all that?"

The accountant, knowing the owner's financials, makes a quick calculation and grimly announces that far from making five cents on each item, he actually would be losing fifteen cents. Recommendation: return the machine.

Did you spot the fallacy in this so-called professional's judgment?

All those accounting costs so elaborately computed will not change whether the machine sits in the corner or is returned. The accountant is wrong; the proprietor has made the right call. The accountant is using stewardship accounting. The owner is using cash accounting, a.k.a., managerial accounting.

The field of managerial accounting rose up after WWII as business schools began expanding broadly and economists were promoting concepts like present value analysis, incremental cost, marginal cost, full cost, relevant cost, and marginal revenue. Instead of focusing on a company's external audiences who needed to be informed about the company's state of affairs, the focus of this new managerial accounting would be on helping managers with their decision-making.

Some Relevant Accounting History

Accounting as we know it first took shape in the thirteenth century with Italian merchants turning to double-entry bookkeeping. This method, which involves recording each transaction in separate accounts, debits and credits, lifted up both the accuracy and reliability of financial records and improved business management.

The widespread adoption of this system was greatly influenced by Luca Pacioli, an Italian mathematician, who in 1494 published *Summa de Arithmetica, Geometria, Proportioni et Proportionalita*. This book provided the first comprehensive description of double-entry bookkeeping and installed Pacioli as the father of accounting.

Over time, accounting practices advanced with the business demands of the unfolding Industrial Revolution. The creation of professional bodies like the Institute of Chartered Accountants in England and Wales and the American Institute of Certified Public Accountants in the nineteenth century standardized practices. The development of GAAP further shaped the field, ensuring consistency and reliability across financial reporting.

However, GAAP is geared to traceability/auditability for the benefit of the owners or shareholders or creditors, those who have "claims" on the company. All that is fine, but for managing the operations of a company, there is another form of accounting, cost accounting.

The two overlap a great deal, but not knowing the differences can materially impact management decisions.

Cost accounting focuses on measuring, recording, and analyzing a company's costs of production. It encompasses the calculation of both fixed and variable costs associated with the production of goods and services. It provides detailed cost information that helps managers assess profitability, control expenses, and set pricing strategies. By examining direct costs like materials and labor, as well as indirect costs such as overhead, cost accounting helps businesses determine the actual cost of each product or service, guiding strategic planning and operational efficiency to improve profitability.

I will give a few examples to highlight the key concepts of cost accounting and contrast it with financial stewardship accounting.

I do recommend taking a short course on accounting—the online curricula are satisfactory. It won't take more than twenty to twenty-five hours, but it will pay off. With basic foundational knowledge, you'll then be able to pick up additional overlays of information with ease as you go. If you don't invest those few hours early on, accounting will always appear too complicated to get involved with, and the financial consequences could become very serious, especially when you're spending more time in negotiations as your LC heads for a Rich Exit. Put differently, there isn't much chance of an RE without getting a handle on basic accounting from the get-go.

Considering the Cost of Production

A product consists of labor and materials and, as appropriate, overhead allocated on a reasonable basis. That's the short form. Getting into this simple costing formula (labor + material cost per unit = product cost) gets complicated with all the variations in practice. These complications can easily get overwhelming unless you equip yourself with ambiguity tolerance along with its traveling partner, judicious simplification.

Let's start with material costs.

The materials are piled next to the workstation. The worker takes five units from the inventory of parts and inserts them into the product, which now moves onto the next workstation. What is the cost of those five units? It depends on the costing system used for the inventory. If parts are being purchased in lots and accumulated, chances are good that each lot will come at a different price. Layers of costs.

Even though the parts might be in one big pile, costing remains layered. If the parts are assumed to come from the earliest lot and costed as such, it is last in, first out (LIFO). If the first lot is assumed to be the first used, it is first in, first out (FIFO). If there has been an inflationary trend, the product material costs could widely fluctuate, making the accounting (as well as the realizing of profits in the period) rather difficult.

It is worth asking how the worker at the workstation is meant to keep track of such costs. Not easily. So often, LIFO and FIFO accounting concerns are thrown out the window, and the parts issued by the stockroom are merely stated at standard costs. Come time for year-end accounting, the actual and standard costs need to be reconciled in variance reports, which can get sticky.

Now on to labor costs.

Typically, the starting point for these is the salary cost per hour of the billable staff, also called the direct staff. That's easy to compute. However, as the staff size grows, so do the number of billing rates to be computed—assuming there is a rate for each, and there usually is. Often, direct staff in similar skill categories (engineer, senior engineer, principal consultant, staff accountant, etc.) are lumped together into buckets with an average salary attached to that bucket and an average cost per hour.

Much like the inventory layers causing cost fluctuations in actual material costing even though the same parts are used, direct labor costs can also fluctuate depending on utilization levels, distorting profit computations and even upsetting clients if they see the billing rates.

For instance, if a direct staff has a low utilization, say ten hours one particular week, the direct labor costs will be high. If those are applied to a product, the product costs will go up. Should they, though? If a client is billed in this case, those ten hours will be at much higher rates. The reverse is true when the staff works sixty hours the following week; the client benefits, and the product costs go down. Clients will surely be confused. Worse, how can project managers control costs if direct labor costs are widely fluctuating and the staff is working on multiple projects simultaneously, each with its own project manager?

In cost accounting, this is dealt with using standard costing. One assumes that the staff will be billable to, say, 70 percent of available hours across a period (typically a year). Then 70 percent of the annual potentially billable hours would be the denominator for the direct labor cost computation, which, when allocated to the hourly rate, would give the standard direct labor cost. At the end of the year, a reconciliation will be made. How the variances are treated is a matter for management to decide. My experience across decades is that if proper statistical methods are used, the variances between standard costs and actual costs at year- or even quarter-end are minimal.

As an aside, for a law firm, the billable hours for the year might be 2,000, and that means the total work hours were likely 2,300 to 2,400 hours. For government work, the annual work hours are assumed to be 2,080, forty hours per week times fifty-two weeks. From this, vacation days, personal days, and sick days, each assumed to be eight hours, are deducted. Typically, 1,850 is the net work hours available for projects, training, conferences, and so on. Now, assuming the 70 percent utilization rate, the billable hours would come to roughly 1,500 per year.

How about overhead like management costs, IT, accounting, legal, facilities, insurance, and so on? Those costs have to be accounted for and reflected in product and labor costs. Especially the labor costs billed to clients. There are many ways of aggregating and then allocating these overhead costs, and the details can get very convoluted, but the principles need not.

First, nonproduction overhead cost pools (such as legal, accounting, IT, HR) are allocated based on a decided metric (such as space occupied or headcount). These pools are then aggregated into one big pool that, when divided by the total anticipated billable hours for the year, yields the overhead rate per direct labor hour. And now the sum of the overhead rate plus the direct labor costs is the total cost per hour. It is then marked up by a profit percentage, and that is the billing rate either to the customer or to a product being built.

Another way is to divide the total overhead pool by the total direct salary cost to come up with a percentage, which then is used to mark up the direct labor costs per hour. Typical overhead rates range from less than 100 percent to more than 200 percent per person. These rates can also be expressed as a multiple. For instance, if the direct labor cost is $50 per hour and the overhead rate is 200 percent, then the total labor cost per hour would be $150 or three times the direct labor cost figure. I'm talking about cost. Profit is not yet included. That profit is context dependent. The government typically allows no more than 10 percent, but in commercial projects, 15 percent to 25 percent is typically used.

Understanding Cost and Price

Costs have a huge bearing on pricing, of course, which is make or break for a young company bringing new product innovations to the marketplace. If pricing is based on assumed costs that are below true costs, no amount of sales will allow profitability (at least for the LC not relying on venture capital to buy market share).

Sometimes it makes sense for an LC to price below cost for a period as part of a deliberate strategy, but not because of miscomputed costs. Conversely, if the computed costs run higher than they are (as with the simple restaurant illustration above), then a great many potential sales could be forsaken simply because the cost-based pricing was thought to be higher than what the market would in fact accept or the competition be offering.

Pricing is so important to an LC that I urge you to focus intensely on it, evolve your own expertise, and consult with pricing experts (an example of when the E in AAWE can pay off). Marketing consultants who focus on pricing theory and strategy are valuable adjuncts and often critical to "getting it right."

Often the knee-jerk approach for pricing is to compute costs and add in the biggest profit margin the market will allow, and that's the price. However, I have long argued that *pricing should be based on value imparted.*

Consider this example. An acre of land is being used as a parking lot on Fifth Avenue in Manhattan. No one would propose selling that acre at cost plus. The right price is the market price. But how to determine that? It requires knowing the cost, for sure, but also the comps, the history, and foremost, the value of the choice plot of land to a potential buyer. If a developer is looking to erect a skyscraper on that acre, then the price is going to rise high, high above the comps.

Value-based pricing is the interplay between data, art, and intuition. (It took me several years, in fact, to find the right balance between cost-based and value-based pricing for my company.) The situation in value-based pricing gets even trickier when the potential buyer knows the cost history (often not hard to find out) and pretends to be taken advantage of (often the tactic taken) if the proposed price is markedly above cost plus a reasonable markup.

In my pricing proposals, when I found myself confronted with the charge that my value-based pricing was unfair or unreasonably high, I would ask a question back: Do you have any shares of stock that have appreciated enormously that you'll sell to me at your acquisition cost plus a markup, even a high markup? That usually triggered a shift in the tenor of conversation, and no, nobody ever sold me any shares of stock for far less than market value. Dang.

This kind of pushback on value-based pricing often occurred from my own company's colleagues. Even from those in sales, amazingly. They couldn't seem to understand how a software company like ours, where the operating margins could run as high as 80 to 90 percent since the software simply needed to be downloaded by the client, could charge so much.

One example of this obstinacy from my own team stood out. Kenan System had developed sophisticated AI-based billing and customer care software for the telecommunications industry. I priced it at $2 million, and a couple of my colleagues blew a gasket over that. They called it price gouging. But was it?

I pointed out that the only alternative for these telecom companies was a custom system since there was no other software on the market—except ours. The vendors of these custom systems included IBM, EDS, and the like. They were charging $20–$100 million for systems that would, in addition, take two to five years to build and install. We could install our system right away, do the data migration in fewer than six months, and get the customer up and running in time periods never seen before. Tremendous value given.

By all rights, we could have priced our software at $10 million but did not. We wanted to expand swiftly through market share as well as make an impact—always the near-background objective for me. So, I held the price firm at $2 million for many years and fair to say, it worked. What we lost from pricing under market value (but still with comfortable margins), we amply made up for in volume.

Clearly, there are many nuances to billing properly and pricing effectively. But we've covered the basics that link accounting, management, production, sales, and marketing in a financial model that is ready to take the LC to primetime.

Hiring the Right Kind of Lawyer

Just as I outlined for building an HR and accounting team from the bottom up using AAWE and repurposing talent from within as much as possible, the legal team should ideally be built up from first your junior hires using AAWE, then engaging outside law firms, and then bringing in specialized legal talent for specific situations.

A junior hire can be a paralegal, as they are well trained in the handling of routine legal matters. The pool of paralegals is large and relatively inexpensive.

I also recommend that an evolving legal department understand the value and practice of disempowerment in their domain.

When hiring for Kenan Systems, I assumed that our legal needs would be as complex as our accounting needs. So, I went for an E (Experience) in hiring a general counsel. Making a hiring decision had become necessary because the outside firms we were using had become cost prohibitive, took too long to turn important documents around, and took to handing our work over to their less savvy junior partners while the talented senior partners spent all their time trying to coax me out to the golf course to upsell me on new services. Yes, for an LS becoming an LC as Kenan Systems was then, it was time to hire a general counsel.

Soon, our E lawyer had maneuvered himself into a position of indispensability. And bingo, he was a general counsel with extensive internal power. As you can now suspect, I had my concerns about this, but I needed to keep focused on finding additional legal talent because our inbox of contracts was overflowing. In time, I would find a team of four more lawyers who checked all the AAWE boxes, but right then, we had a far-from-ideal contracts process in place.

Traditional Contracts versus Peace Contracts

When a deal would approach the contractual stage, my general counsel would give me a draft contract that I would present to the prospective client. Time after time, we would get bogged down in the more "confrontational" clauses of the draft contract. It became maddening, even. I would have to send posthaste instructions back to our general counsel to modify those clauses on the basis that we had no intention of ever suing a client—except in a case of blatant fraud. At one point, with the end of my rope in sight, I decided that what we needed instead were peace contracts.

My general counsel's response to that was to state that I didn't understand how the law works.

Be that as it may, I said, as the CEO, could I draft a model peace contract for legal to tweak and polish?

He pushed back on the same grounds but realized he couldn't stop me.

When lawyers write contracts, they typically fill the body of the contract with the so-called T&Cs, the terms and conditions (such as warranty, liability, breach, termination, and assignability). Then they take the real core of the contract (the SOW, or statement of work, associated deliverables, and schedules) and relegate those pieces to an appendix. Since the lawyers are rarely in a position to deliver that core information, the appendix is often left blank in the drafting stage.

I wanted the SOW in the body of the contract and the T&Cs in the appendix.

I also wanted the T&Cs to be fair and easy to understand.

In taking this approach, I would be able to negotiate the SOW with the client's technical and management staff and exclude the lawyers from those discussions—where they contributed little anyway.

In these company head to company head negotiations, we could settle on the SOW, the deliverables, schedules, acceptance clauses, price, and payment schedule. I could then couple those business terms with our standard peace-oriented T&Cs in an attachment for the client's lawyers to review.

This coupling became a powerful way to subsequently negotiate the T&Cs with the lawyers, who were often bent on fiercely advocating for their clients at the risk of jeopardizing the deal (a byproduct of an empowered legal team). Since our terms were truly fair, often their legal team would go along. When they did push back, I would have a counterargument at the ready.

With one major company, I negotiated all the business terms and made a lot of progress in the T&Cs, except for the warranty. We were offering our technology *as is*, and therefore there would be no warranties. The matter was escalated to their head of legal. My business contact at the company told me legal would never budge on this.

I countered that a warranty is a form of insurance. If his company wanted a warranty, then I would increase the price by 10 percent to buy an insurance policy to cover the warrant risks. Or else they could take the price I offered and do their own risk management. In this case, that 10 percent represented a substantial sum since the contract was into millions of dollars. And I pointed out to the client that typically the legal department wants to minimize risk but does not want that minimization to increase costs.

My proposal was going to clearly increase the costs based entirely on their legal department's position. He laughed at me and said that nonetheless he had never seen his legal budge. So, I told him there would be no deal. We came to a standstill. I informed my colleagues that this deal was dead. Nobody was happy.

Somehow, a few days later, my contact called to say that his legal team had suddenly seen the light and had backed off. We signed the multimillion-dollar contract.

In all my negotiations, I followed the approach of handling the SOW and the business terms first, and then proceeding to the T&Cs. In one case, I fondly recall concluding the deal so swiftly that in the final meeting, I told the CEO and his assembled executives that everything had gone so smoothly precisely because no lawyers had been allowed to join us at the negotiating table. You could hear a pin drop, as they say. After a long pause, the CEO informed me that he was a lawyer. More silence. Me, red faced. Only then did the CEO politely signal that he was a reformed lawyer who appreciated my presenting them with peace contracts that were fair to both sides.

Starting a Project at the Real Start

In working with clients of any size, it is invariably wise to resist starting work on the project until the ink is dry on the contract. Several things can and often muck things up. An unsigned contract is truly not binding unless/until taken to court. I was once knocked sideways into that learning.

I'd struck a deal with an executive at a big client. Their legal green-lighted the contract, though it was not yet formally signed. We jumped into the project, scoping it out, excited for the challenge. A couple of weeks later, the executive was visiting our offices, and I asked him to show a little commitment to the deal. He smiled, went over to my office whiteboard, and scrawled out his signature. "Work for you?" he asked. I nodded, knowing I should have been more circumspect. But based on that signature, we officially got working on what was a very big project.

A couple more weeks passed, and still I had no formally signed documents.

Then we heard that the executive had a falling-out with his CEO and would be leaving the company. His replacement had zero interest in the project. When I lamely pointed to the signature on my whiteboard, he practically howled with laughter. I found that laughter deafening. Our company took a big hit, and a lesson was learned.

My father had a favorite saying among his many. Once burnt from hot milk, you'll then blow on anything white to cool it down. After that abrupt project cancellation, I put a big Post-it Note on my computer: *Insist on a signed contract before beginning work.* And the deliverables schedule was predicated on the contract-signing date being day zero and subsequent time segments extending out from there.

No matter how small or big the contract, or how raring the team is to get going on the project, prudence demands signed documents with the SOW and delivery dates all predicated on the contract date.

Only once after that whiteboard stunt did I break this rule. A major company's CTO had chosen to go with our system and made it clear that if the system was not up and running by year's end, the company might lose its license. I agreed to start at once since otherwise we could not meet the deadline. But I asked for two conditions.

First, that we be paid a substantial amount up front with the remainder upon installation. And second, that the contract be signed within a month. I sent one of our lawyers to meet with their lawyers— who were an outside firm. They got hung up on what I considered a minor matter and would not budge. So, I went directly to the company's

CTO, and together we tried to knock some sense into the lawyer. We failed. Nonetheless, we worked on and delivered the system on time and on budget, and got fully paid, but still no sign-off from the lawyer.

In our last meeting, I confronted the lawyer, telling him that in his efforts presumably to protect his client from every conceivable downside risk, he had now exposed his client to a huge risk. The system was installed and running. We had been fully paid. Since there was no contract, the company had no protection at all. None. I could walk away right there, but I certainly did want to resolve any remaining issues as a matter of honor. His response was, "I will take all that under advisement." That was my last interaction with him.

Back to the hot milk, if I may. I think we all develop our own rules of thumb based on the most dramatic and trying experiences we've faced. I call these our "ghosts from the past." These ghosts can transform the way we act in existential ways, altering our reactions to things from flexible to rigid, turning old views on things practically into shibboleths, taking little misconceptions to the point of superstition. Case in point:

Once sitting around a negotiation table, I could sense that all of us seemed to have these ghosts operating beneath the surface. So, I said as much, and invited everyone on both sides of the deal to recognize their ghosts and resolve to leave them all behind. For a long moment, I could sense some hostility to the idea all around the table. But then a colleague on the other side admitted she'd had a bad experience with a small resource-constrained company and agreed to not conflate my small company with that bad experience.

I then admitted that we had been bullied more than once by a big company, but I would not assume that this big company would do the same. As others joined in, a cathartic lightness spread around the table, soon we were talking freely and negotiating deal terms, as if we were old friends. That little exercise made a big difference that day.

There is a corollary note of caution for an LC negotiating with a big Fortune 500-type company that has multiple divisions, all involved in the deal and eager to press their special interests on the deal. It is important in this situation to take the time to find out who's on first and what's on second, as it were. For the small company, it's usually WYSIWYG.

But on the big company side of the table, there are at least three key parties representing a multitude of interests. There are the technical people working out the SOW and deliverables. There is the contracting negotiator focused on the commercial terms. Then there are the lawyers hammering away on the T&Cs. Each go-round with each of these three parties can slice and dice the deal in some new way. So, how best to figure out these three parties' primary interests in order to best approach each one?

Technical wants a broad scope and quick deliverables even though that can translate into higher prices.

Contracting is expert at squeezing the price.

Legal may tack on innocuous-looking clauses that could be costly—such as warranties and unreasonable acceptance clauses.

Handling each party's specific interest within the context of the overall deal will move the negotiation along more smoothly.

There is often another round that can be devastating: final executive approval. Executives, being executives, can unravel carefully negotiated pieces of the contract with a swish of the red pen. Then it's back to the table. Or it could be that the proposed project price doesn't fit their budgets or is above their signature levels, which means the project now needs to be kicked upstairs (often another word for purgatory). In the meantime, at your LC, the clock is ticking, payables are overdue, and payroll is fast approaching.

Having seen this C-suite scenario play out more than once, I made it a point to determine the decision-making processes of a prospective client going in, identifying each key player as keenly as possible, and then drawing the circle and the cross.

I also asked prospective clients about budgets and budget cycles—for they can be the bearers of so many unpleasant surprises. Most often the case was the client wanted to negotiate a good deal and get it all done right away, but alas, it had to fit into the next budget cycle—which was a year out. So, it's better to surface this information early on and deal with it realistically so you're not stuck building out unrealistic revenue projections.

Developing on Limited Resources

Our thesis is that an LC can enjoy an RE by following a proven set of principles and business guidelines. So, a big question at each step along the way, given that the company is running lean, is how to best allocate what will always be strictly limited resources.

Is it better to dedicate them to development and production, for example, or to sales and marketing? My recommendation is both, and in a way that interlinks them. As for some perspective on this ...

First, a perspective on the customer. I view a customer as a cus-tom-er—a source of customs or habits, if you will. A model customer can imprint good habits on an LC and be a rich source of learnings. Conversely, an unethical or aggressive customer can imprint these bad habits onto an LC, which in time become part of the company's fabric, even its moral fabric.

A good customer that's well established and respected in the industry that the LC is targeting can be a great role model for shaping the LC's development and ultimately its practices. I call this client-driven development.

For an LC that has acquired its staff through AAWE, the linkages to the client could indeed lead to enormous learnings. Teach and learn, learn and teach internally, and also do so with the clients.

Even in a classroom setting, the professor who engages with students and tries to learn from them will benefit greatly. In the olden days, the primary sources of learning for students were classroom lectures and textbooks. Hours were spent in the library.

Now, each student, through the infinite reach of the internet, has almost immediate access to relevant knowledge. It is not uncommon during a lecture for the professor to be confronted by a student who just has done an online search and found the professor on a wrong, usually outdated track. Why get annoyed with this? Why not turn each student into a node of research and engage in collective teach and learn, learn and teach?

It works similarly in client-driven development. Allow a client to become a teacher as well as a recipient of your company's expertise. If your own expertise is sufficiently strong, no amount of expertise on the client side can threaten you, only enlighten you.

Delivering the Product

In the early days of an LC, most hours are usually spent in development. It is an interesting time, an exciting time that, by its nature, is tolerant of errors. Before any product has gone out the door, weaknesses can be overcome, errors corrected. But all tolerance goes away when deliveries begin.

These first deliveries are immensely consequential and can make or break the evolving company. More so in the era of real-time evaluations, ratings, and rankings from many sources, not just clients. Since the track record of the LC is not yet established, one delivery gone awry can be hard to recover from.

An example from academia: A bad grade from a course during the freshman year can really mess up the year's grade point average. It might take until the junior year and lots of good grades to finally overcome that freshman-year mess-up. But if the GPA is solid through the junior year and in the senior year there's a single mess-up, its effect will be minimal. Real-world analog: While IBM and Microsoft can survive one messed-up client engagement, an LC may not.

So, how to establish a solid track record of development and delivery?

The starting point is to negotiate good contracts. *Contracts are the pillars of an* LS *and* LC *aiming for an* RE. If the contract promises deliverables that will be a stretch or potentially unattainable, then failure is highly likely. If the financial terms set out in the contract are onerous, then the company's resources will be stretched thin, perhaps too thin since there may be no offsetting cash coming in during the development period.

Let's illustrate this principle with an innocuous-looking clause in a contract: *Acceptance, with a Big Payment Tied to Acceptance.*

Many LSs and even some LCs will fall for this one. After all, what's not to like about a big payment coming from the client when they accept the product?

Well, what exactly does the word *acceptance* mean? And who is deciding that? If you are uninvolved in the contract, you might not realize that the client cleverly left that open ended. Your product will then be completed and delivered, but the client has not accepted it and hence will not pay for it, even though they are using it. And worse, they may continue finding "issues" with it that need to be corrected before acceptance. It's a road to free improvements for the client and a road to ruin for you.

Prudence demands a carefully worded acceptance plan in the contract with a backstop, as well: acceptance to be completed in X days, and if the product is put into use, it is deemed accepted after Y days, preferably immediately.

Development Staff

If the development team has been hired using AAWE, it's likely the client-driven development will occur in due course. Same for teach and learn, learn and teach with the client. I found that AAWE-based teams possess more of the audacity and courage required to try new paths. There are, however, downsides to AAWE hires that may need to be mitigated.

For one, the error rate of an inexperienced team is usually higher. Soon the error rate will moderate as the boost from A and A and W propel productivity and quality higher. So, having quality assurance and tracking with metrics can be very helpful, especially since the first A and fast learning overlap nicely.

And second, AAWEs are going to be more excited by the drive to perfection. Earlier, we talked about the ideal of perfection, specifically the differences between *best* and *excellence,* and now the best of an average effort is still average, so it is excellence that must be sought.

However, a young development team can easily confuse excellence with perfection and keep pushing on and on. And in so doing, the product remains in the development phase long after it was supposed to be delivered. No delivery, no cash.

This is when you don the implementation hat and lay down firm deadlines. I found it useful to enforce deadlines with some more company vocabulary.

When developers are informed that they are "now tinkering," the point gets across rapidly, and the burden of proof shifts to them. Before they may have thought that anything less than the very best is cheating the client; now they realize that the configuration, reconfiguration, or deconfiguration they were so wedded to may hurt delivery, in turn hurting the client and the company as well.

Letting Go to Delivery

So, yes, it's good to have an eye for the developer turned tinkerer. It's even more important to recognize a potential rub in things as a product moves from development to delivery.

Development managers tend to be Y-types: team-oriented, consensus minded, tolerant of delays and errors. But delivery requires more of an X-type manager. So, there's the rub. It can be hard for a development manager to hand over the product to a differently minded person *unless* the practice of situational leadership is an accepted part of the culture and each team member knows when it is time for another to take the reins of leadership.

Shortsighted Professionalism

From the CEO's perspective, the overall picture is often quite clear. The objective is to go from point A to point B, and in there close to the start is the development stage. All very clear to the CEO. But often less so to the development staff. I'll illustrate this graphically.

Say point A is at the origin of a graph and point B is at forty-five degrees, and the shortest path is a straight line at forty-five degrees. To the CEO, that is the way to go on the project. But for the director of development, this looks like a crooked line since she sees only her segment of the project. She tries to make her segment a horizontal line, and it turns into a blockage.

When confronted about this, she might say earnestly that her professional ethics prevent her from working on crooked matters. You can then show her the whole project strategy, but sometimes there are risks in sharing the whole thing, and what's more, it can be very time-consuming. So, beware that what is straight at the top level can be seen crooked locally.

I've had many such encounters. In one of them, I was involved in a three-way sale. There was the implementation partner, the ultimate client who would buy the system, and our company with our offer. Our strategy was to have the implementation partner join us to test our offer at the client site. So far, so good.

But as it turned out, our implementation partner had a similar offer they wanted to test right alongside our offer, and they had convinced our company's lead on the project that it made sense to test both. To me, that was a big no-no. But our lead claimed it was the "ethical thing to do." I was stunned. I asked him which company he worked for. He held his ground. Since he had made the matter one of ethics, I decided to back off. Both systems were presented to the client and at our expense, no less. Fortunately, our system prevailed.

Later, I just happened to walk into a meeting where there was plenty of yelling going on, the long and short of which was, our implementation partner had willfully manipulated our lead by convincing him the two-system comparison was the ethical thing to do when it was nothing of the sort. Lesson learned.

Often, in staff meetings, I would draw the A-to-B strategy line and tell the staff that their segment might look crooked only because they didn't have a global perspective. With an inexperienced but capable staff, this is a good lesson to learn early on.

Documentation: A Cornerstone of Success

Development engineers are not known for their documentation skills. Yet I have found that producing top-drawer documentation is the very foundation of a technical company's success, right next to contracts.

Let me explain why and then describe the many uses of well-conceived, well-crafted documentation.

In the early stages of Kenan Systems, I headed up our documentation efforts for the simplest of reasons—I rather enjoyed it. I didn't yet know that it would become one of the cornerstones of our success as a company.

I would coordinate the work of each of our systems development people, taking all their functional specifications and turning them into instruction manuals, systems walk-throughs, user tutorials, maintenance directives—all the how-to that would be needed both by our clients and by our teams.

There are byproducts to every experience, and in this one I found myself gaining a firmer understanding of the talents and skills of each one of our developers. That proved very helpful in assigning projects to the best-suited among them going forward. Even more importantly, it gave me a deep understanding of the functionality of our various systems so that when I went out into the field to sell them, I was much more effective at it.

What's more, I was better primed to conduct noisy explorations with our prospective clients, because my breadth of knowledge about our systems' capability potential mapped to a wider and deeper array of potential-need cases our clients were experiencing.

Along the way, though, I had a delicate experience with this. One of our developers who was aces in coding was also aces in documentation, and fussy about detail. So fussy that one day he stormed into my office, his face a portrait in indignation, and he announced his immediate resignation. Caught me totally off guard. He informed me that he had just seen the documentation draft I had sent to the client, and it had spelling errors and bad grammar to boot, and he simply could not work for a company where the CEO held such low standards.

Still startled by this outburst, I tried to explain that it was only a draft and sent to get the client's feedback. He was not mollified. I had to think of something fast. It hit me, and I asked if he would agree to review what I wrote before it went out. That satisfied him, barely. And I took this lesson to heart, adding a policy and principle from there on out: *All documents leaving the office get a second set of eyes.*

To this day, I still follow this practice on any document of importance.

A few years later, I ran into the flip-side trouble. We'd just hired a bright talent who also had years of top-notch marketing experience. He was composing a letter to send to all our clients, and so I suggested he get it reviewed by some of his colleagues. He too blew up, taking my comment as mistrust in him. He was so emotional that he was about to storm out of my office just as in the first encounter my colleague had stormed in! But I moved fast to better acquaint him with the origins of what had become policy at Kenan Systems—getting a second set of eyes—and he calmed back down. In due time, he came to see the value of the practice.

As my schedule filled to the bursting point at Kenan Systems, it became necessary to transition documentation to someone, but to whom?

It would have been natural to turn the task over to one of the developers. Several of them were excellent writers, but they too were flat out. Why not use AAWE to hire a liberal arts graduate right out of school? They typically have excellent writing skills. With a high aptitude and an open mind to learning, why couldn't they come up to speed in documenting even a highly technical system? I can tell you that many on the team were dubious of the idea. But we did *use AAWE for documentation specialists as well,* and enjoyed a level of success I never could have anticipated.

Rapid Prototyping

In the early stages, both development and delivery can be done by the same teams. As the LS evolves into an LC with many projects underway, there is an advantage to having a delivery team that is more implementation oriented and comfortable with direct client interaction (and good at it).

It's always an advantage if development is client driven, with a top-notch delivery team serving as the bridge between the developers and the client. And there is, in my view, an ideal way to groom this delivery team for race day.

That grooming begins well before the development phase, when the team is in knowledge-gathering mode. Ideally and in our case, the team members would go knowledge gathering at the client's site in what we called split-suiting.

They'd arrive in coat and tie to talk with end users about their functional needs.

Changing into nerd wear, they'd talk with the analysts in accounting, legal, and finance about the models and metrics that could make or break the system.

Then in ripped jeans and T-shirts—granted, their favorite—our split-suiters talked to IT about best integrating our planned systems with existing systems.

Lastly, these three bases of knowledge were folded into a single coherent project description. And we were ready to go, almost.

If our split-suiters did their job well, they formed an excellent bridge between our two companies. And the client would keenly recognize the value of rapidly prototyping the system together with us in a client-centric manner.

Let's look at a sample system development project in context, to see how this approach can work for almost any major project.

The end user's requirements, as captured by the knowledge-engineering team, are converted into a functional spec that then can be the basis for a rapid prototype created in a high-level language, product sketch, or model.

The prototype is then shown to the end users, analysts, and IT. Each offers feedback from their respective viewpoints, and the team goes back to begin making modifications accordingly.

The system is now constructed with the documentation evolving alongside.

For physical product development, the equivalent concept is to prototype the "looks like" part and separately build the "works like" part, which embodies the functional description. Merging the two yields the full prototype, which is then engineered for delivery.

Right Kind of Development Environment

It is natural for developers to desire the most powerful state-of-the-tech development environment the company can afford. Developers yearn for it, and many CEOs go along on the assumption that it promotes productivity. How could it not?

Well, it can surely boost the team's productivity, but at what cost?

When developers take advantage of powerful computing capabilities, they create a system that hums along in the shop. But then they take it to the client's environment, which is rarely as well provisioned, and it's like running into a wall of molasses. "When things crawl, clients bawl," I said to one of our engineers once when he wanted us to buy the newest-latest-fastest-etc. He didn't laugh, and I didn't care. A spartan development environment not only makes more sense; it saves the company lots of money.

An alternative approach which, in fact, does boost productivity if the funds are there is to keep a robust development environment but also duplicate the client's environment to test-drive in.

Personally, I prefer the first alternative since it aligns with the *do more with less* principle. And it's certainly easy enough later in the life of an LC to beef up development tools and also create a test bed to mimic the client's environment.

First Client Success, Then Client Satisfaction

In today's vernacular, the pursuit of client satisfaction, even client delight, is all the rage. But not in my view—as experienced in both academia and business.

In academia, the student is the client, so let's look at that situation. Sadly, this is both an illustrative story and the state of things at some schools.

Classes begin, and the students begin complaining about the cost of the textbooks. So, to make them "happy," the professor decrees no textbooks and passes out notes to all. After a few weeks of homework, students are again displeased. Homework sucks, they insist. So, to make them happy, the professor writes the problem sets on the whiteboard and provides the solution sets. Next comes exam time, and students complain that taking exams could trigger them. So, the professor nixes the exams. And clearly getting less than a B+ will not do. You can guess how the professor grades. The course ends, and the students are at last happy. However, in the course evaluation the students rate it as a mick or gut course—fun but little learned. More serious students call it a waste of time.

Contrast this with a professor who puts student learning above student satisfaction. Lectures are hard, textbooks mandatory, exams are frequent and tough, there are pop quizzes, lab work, and term papers, and class participation matters. Student satisfaction drops as the course progresses. Relevance is questioned. Some drop out. But at the end of the term, students have learned. And they appreciate the course all the more in their first skirmishes with the real world of business. They communicate as much back to the professor when they return to alumni events.

I suspect you know which of these approaches I championed at MIT!

Another example is the doctor who adopts the "delight your customer" mantra. One of her patients really loves cigarettes. No problem, she says, we'll deal with the consequences when they come up. The patient wants to eat junk food and is putting on weight. No problem, there are drugs for that. The patient is lying in a hospital bed, dying, pointing an angry finger at the doctor for sending him to an early grave. The doctor pleads, "But I kept you delighted!"

While these examples skate toward caricature, their equivalents in systems and product development are very real. At the launch of the project, both the probability of success and the client's expected satisfaction are high. If the guiding objective is client satisfaction, many requests will be accommodated, some even without change orders. The system will get bloated. Bugs will appear and then accumulate. Costs will escalate. But hey, the client is happy; his requests are all being readily adopted. He is looking forward to a successful launch of this system in his offices … though the chances of a timely launch are becoming less and less likely. When at the end, the system is wobbly and runs slowly and costs are out of line, the client who was delighted during development is now bitter and angry.

In my view, *client success should be the foremost objective.* Clients should be managed tactfully along the way with a sufficient number of "sorry, we cannot do that" and "but that will substantially increase your costs" conversations. There are many ways to push back that will be seen, even if begrudgingly, as being in the client's best interests. And then, after the successful delivery on time and on budget, with the client now marveling at the capability of the system, the wisdom of this approach will be even more obvious to the client. As will their interest now in looking at some of the add-ons that you had said no to but that can now be approached on a reasoned schedule.

Productization

As a new company, an LS will usually be focused on deliverables with limited appeal or customized one-off solutions. This narrow focus is entirely normal and appropriate since the company's first set of deliverables is still in need of maturing, client feedback, market validation, and competitive responses before they can hope to find their place as legitimate solutions in the marketplace where they are then valued by many. But when that time comes, when a company's one-off begins showing promise as a repeatable product, this is the time when the LS can become an LC and no longer a service-centric company.

This is the most difficult of transitions for companies, and most fail for several reasons. I will address some of the key ones.

Transitions from *custom* to *product* tend to happen when customer success has taken root as a guiding principle. If customer success takes a back seat to customer accommodation, chances are that the delivered product will be a one-off that is highly tailored and possibly bloated and not a good candidate for platforming and rolling out the offers widely—that is, productizing the offers.

For going from custom to product, think core and shell.

The core of the thing will remain unchanged from engagement to engagement; it is the essential bit. It could be an invention, an algorithm, IP, whatever. The shell is the customizable part of the thing that changes with each project to meet the specific needs of the customer. Initially the core may be small compared to the shell. But iterations of deliveries help the core grow in size, capability, and market value.

For expanding the core, think building blocks, like Lego blocks. As the core expands with these blocks, the shell can be continually adapted to meet the different needs of different engagements. As well, the price you charge can go down since COGS has. This opens up more sales opportunities leading to more engagements, which in turn build out the core blocks.

This core-and-shell thinking is aided by the creation of first-rate documentation. This documentation must now strive to make the client as independent of the company as possible. Some LSs fall into the temptation of making the client dependent so as to generate more service revenue. That may be fine in the short term, but not for becoming an LC poised for that RE.

Infighting over Productization

While building a company platform with core-and-shell building blocks can occur logically through customer engagements, at one point it makes more sense to put a dedicated productization team in place. This is far easier said than done.

At Kenan Systems, we chose to divide the company into two groups: the custom group and the productization group. The custom group continued to generate revenue with billable hours and steady deliveries, while the productization group absorbed the resources needed to build the company's future.

More than once, I spied folks on the custom side gazing across the office at the productization group, looking at it like you would a sinkhole that swallowed up your house, your car, all you care about. And not just resources but talented peers were disappearing into the sinkhole, no longer available to help on projects they cared about. It was hard to watch and harder to handle when it all came to a head.

The custom group became overbooked and was laboring under intense pressure to hit deadlines. They would see their very capable colleagues sitting across the office but unavailable to them in their time of need. They would lobby me to borrow staff for "just a while." They would outright steal younger colleagues who felt afraid to say no to these senior performers. They would keep pushing their case because they felt desperate. But I could not give in—because unless we successfully productized, we could not survive as a company, much less grow it.

One of the more corrosive arguments the custom group put to me was, "We earn the revenue; they spend it." Even more corrosive was, "I earned the revenue with my wildly successful projects, and you, the CEO, are spending that revenue elsewhere. Not right."

My first encounter with this kind of "I made it happen, so the results are mine" attitude was very early on. I had personally hired six MBAs out of MIT—all technically savvy and well trained. Ideal colleagues in all ways, fitting AAWE to a T and excellent at split-suiting. Together we accomplished a lot.

That said, I was at the time carrying a somewhat herculean burden as the founder/CEO, as the person roaming the world to find multimillion-dollar projects, as the one sweating out tough contract negotiations, as the one meeting the payroll, dealing with taxes, carrying the legal, accounting, and HR functions, and even coming at night to clean the offices (with my son's help). All that they saw not so clearly. What they saw, as the developers of our systems, was that "their systems made the company."

I had formed an executive committee with these original six hires, and every month I would take them out to dinner to celebrate. At one such dinner meeting, I had to step out to make a call. When I came back, I was informed that they had made "an executive decision," and since we all seven were making things happen, they had decided that the company shares (which I held alone) would be (*not should be, but would be*) divided seven ways, with me getting the "lion's share."

I kept my lion's cool and donned my professorial hat for the lecture on capitalism they seemed to have missed at MIT. It was a lengthy tutorial. Among the questions I put to them was this: How would it work if the management of, say, GM or IBM or AT&T thought the same way, and on the grounds that they run the company and bring in the revenue and the shareholders are just there to collect the benefits, they should move their company's shares into their personal accounts, never mind those of the stockholders?

I think our young group of technical geniuses had their eyes opened, and before the meal ended, we had moved beyond the "takeover attempt."

I had another encounter years later. I had personally recruited and hired an excellent graduate from a premier school. He performed extremely well. At the time, I was doing all the performance reviews. After we went through the preliminaries, he said he had an important question. He had found out that his billing rate was three times his salary. Indeed, our overhead plus markup was 200 percent of the base salary for the technical staff. He wondered what I was doing with that huge "profit" he was bringing to the company over and beyond his salary. He wanted to have a hand in how it was all spent!

Instead of getting upset or annoyed, I set out to teach him and learn from what he was aiming to teach me, erroneous as that teaching might seem to me, for clearly he believed in what he was saying.

So, I went through the first erroneous part, the multiple. I detailed each component, such as rent, utilities, support costs, property taxes, insurance, indirect materials, etc., and taught him how these components are rolled up into the overhead pool, which then gets methodically allocated to the billable staff. He was astounded. He had no idea, but his W was strong, and he quickly latched on to the ideas of gross and net margin—giving him an entirely different view of his contribution to revenue.

Then I got into who owns the revenue. I proposed a thought exercise: that he set himself up as a company and see if he could get the projects and the resultant revenue he thought he was earning and belonged to him. Would the client really award him the same kinds of contracts, with him now being a solo operator? Not likely.

Even if he got the contracts, now he'd have to provide the development, the delivery, rent for his space, utilities, insurance, taxes, etc., and allocate the time for sales and marketing so he could stay in business. We concluded that, if operating on his own, he would be lucky to match his current salary of $50,000. That encounter led to the following principle:

Revenue is for the company, by the company, and therefore of the company.

In many companies, this kind of thinking might not happen at the individual level, but it does at the group level. That is what the CEO encounters when the all-important product group is being established, yet an office full of talented people still views the product project as a sinkhole.

So, it is a good idea early on to embed in the company culture the idea (which in a capitalist nation shouldn't be hard to grasp, but still somehow is) that the company as a whole earns the revenue. It is like legs saying they do the walking. Yes, but only together with the rest of the body, each body part contributing.

Despite my best efforts to mediate the intramural fight raging in our offices, the custom group persisted in its confrontations with the productization group. Frustrated and desperate for any guidance they might offer, I went to the board. I knew that each of them had managed multidivisional companies; surely, they would have ideas. Their recommendation: Move the productization group to another location—out of sight, out of mind.

I did, and it worked.

Value of Middle-out Thinking

When wrestling with a big decision to be made, how do you approach it?

Some like to start at the top level or top line, aiming to crisp the thesis or get the big picture right and then drill down into the details of the thing.

Others prefer a bottom-up approach, getting the underlying factors identified and then working up to a plan before proceeding.

Whether the approach taken is top to bottom or bottom to top, the risk these two approaches share is that the process can take a while, and surprises can pop up in the interim, upsetting carefully thought-through plans.

For this reason, I have sometimes turned to a third approach, middle-out thinking. The idea here is to start from the most convenient departure point, and as you move forward, look up to figure out the top line and look down to identify the details, all while iterating, learning, teaching, and doing noisy explorations coupled with judicious simplification and a healthy dose of ambiguity and uncertainty tolerance. It can be a powerful approach.

A good example of this principle is walking—yes, walking, which requires more planning than you might first imagine. Because no matter how detailed your plan for walking is, once in effect it needs to be dynamically altered in context lest you smash into a wall or tumble off a cliff you initially did not see. And if you do decide to make detailed plans for your walk, you may end up spending an inordinate amount of time planning each step along your intended route and not have enough time left to actually get out and walk to your destination—which, after all, is the primary objective.

Another common example is business meeting presentations. You may have planned everything to a T for a meeting that will start at 10:30 with the key executive and her staff. You have rehearsed ten times and feel confident that in the allotted forty-five minutes, you will cover every point and have time for questions. You arrive well before the meeting, but now the key executive is held up in traffic, and she comes thirty minutes late, leaving you only fifteen minutes. Have you prepared for this possibility ahead of time (because it does happen)?

We could go on with examples of the value of middle-out thinking, but the point is made. So, let's push on to sales and marketing. Without it, there is no path forward from an LS to an LC.

Sales and Marketing: An Unorthodox Model

When I entered the business world to test the validity of my teachings and pontifications, I had suppositions to prove out such as AAWE, noisy explorations, split-suiting, functional descriptions rather than specifications, rapid iterative prototyping, parallel documentation, success-based client satisfaction, managing via situational leadership, being a jack-of-all-trades, and the CEO/founder not owning the company, but rather a financial interest and working for the company. But in the realm of sales and marketing, I had not yet evolved any suppositions or models, much less any principles.

A few encounters with reality would resolve that.

For quite a while, I was our company's one-man sales and marketing team, able to bring in big custom projects to keep the company going until the point that our customized systems transitioned into a line of products. When that happened, we needed a sales staff.

Marketing was not yet in the picture because I viewed marketing as advertising, publicity, and public relations—not as critical as sales, or so I thought. I was to soon change my mind and in so doing, fashion a rather unorthodox operating model.

But at that time, lacking any point of reference, I used a traditional hiring model. I brought aboard salespeople who found the leads and converted them into sales. Not yet having a sales manager, I ended up crafting the sales team's compensation plans, only then realizing that they are as fundamental to sales as documentation is to development and productization.

Sales Staff Compensation Plans

While the compensation plans for salespeople come in all shapes and sizes, there are core matters of consequence. Just as with HR, legal, and accounting, there are fundamentals that are not hard to learn and must, in fact, be learned.

Typically, compensation plans specify the products or services to be sold and their prices. A salesperson is given a territory to go out into, find leads, and convert them to sales. Traditionally, one salesperson remained on premises to generate leads and handle incoming leads. Today, a company can operate exclusively with banks of salespeople at the company or working from their home offices.

The simplest compensation plan is salary plus a periodic bonus based on management evaluation. However, when there are multiple territories and multiple offers, the plans become more complex and often are commission based. A common structure is as follows:

- Period of performance, often a quarter
- Portfolio of offers included
- Sales targets for each

- Territories
- Base salary
- Commission structure
- How the salesperson will be paid (upon contract signing, when funds are received, etc.)
- How often the above components can be changed, and by whom

Since sales-staff turnover can be high, a question soon arises: What happens if a salesperson leaves the company while a deal is still open, a contract not signed? Are all potential commissions lost upon departure, after ninety days, or what? Compensation plans need to be explicit on these terms.

If the LC has well-defined offers with well-established pro forma contracts, then a simple compensation plan can be utilized easily enough. However, if there are many custom features and the terms and conditions need to be negotiated, then the CEO ought to be involved—especially if there is no sales manager. Even if there is one, certain clauses pertaining to IP, acceptance, warranty, and payment schedules are so consequential that you should make a point of reviewing every contract.

Even a few minutes might be sufficient if you know the key provisions and hence can quickly home in on them. I have negotiated with some large companies, and even they require that key clauses (IP ownership, liability, confidentiality, assignment, etc.) be approved at the highest levels. So, if their top management can find time ...

These seemingly legal issues are actually part and parcel of the sales plan. You need to reserve the right in the compensation plan to reject a deal if the T&Cs are not what you can live with. Otherwise, when you push back after the fact, you'll surely encounter howls of protest, as sales staff can be quite vocal and generally very focused on their compensation. After-the-deal objections are seen as your depriving them of "putting food on the table." I actually got told that by a salesperson whose compensation was astronomical and the deal I was objecting to wouldn't lead to much of a commission. More on that later.

The total compensation is the so-called base pay and the commissions earned. So, how to set the base pay? There are arguments for setting it high as well as low. If the salesperson is really good, does she need a base? But then until commissions come in, how is she going to earn a living? One way the base versus commission question is handled is to give an advance against commissions. So, the starting compensation is the base plus the advance (basically a loan). As the commissions come in, they are used to pay the loan. I think this creates unnecessary complications. Also, what happens if the person leaves before the advance is paid back?

Setting sales revenue targets is a consequential matter. It is a foundation upon which revenue projections are made and the company is organized to compete. And invariably, these targets become sensitive subjects. The salesperson wants low targets and the company quite the opposite. Finding a win-win compromise that is in everyone's best interests becomes one-third art form, one-third analysis, one-third correcting on the fly.

In a base-pay-plus-commission plan, sometimes no commission is earned until the target is achieved. The thinking is that for the base pay, the salesperson should deliver the target sales and earn commissions only if the target is exceeded. Once the target is reached, the commission rate is changed. If the company wishes to goose sales, driving up the rate can accomplish that. But it can also produce unmanageable sales, creating backlogs, delivery issues, etc. Again, art + analysis + correcting.

How the salesperson is paid is also a sensitive and often contentious matter. For the company, it's usually best done on a cash basis—when the customer actually pays, instead of accrual—when the revenue is booked. It's quite the opposite for the salesperson who figures her pay is due on the day of contract signing. In my experience, using a cash basis is better for paying commissions. It has the added benefit of ensuring the salesperson will keep chasing the customer to pay their bill.

If the portfolio has multiple offers, then the easiest things to sell will be the things that sold before. If the offer mix has both mature winners as well as risky new offers that may require extra effort to sell, predictably the new offers will be ignored by sales. This will lead some to conclude that the offers are unsalable, when of course that is not the case. This becomes a roadblock for the company because it is only through introducing innovative new offers that an LC can grow and advance in the marketplace.

Many innovative offers fail in the market *not* because they lack potential but because the sales staff were not properly incentivized to sell with all the energy they're capable of. If new product introductions are central to the LC's future, as they usually are, then a savvy strategy is to assign one very well-incentivized salesperson or group to specialize in these introductions.

I saw this failure of innovation when I joined Lucent Technologies, of all places. Bell Labs would produce an amazing array of innovative but untested offers. But then the centralized sales force and the business groups as well would uniformly shun these new offers. I was startled when a Lucent group president told me that he never trusted anything coming out of Bell Labs.

Flabbergasted, I asked why.

"Because they never really work," he said.

My translation of his words: New products from Bell Labs don't work the first time because they are, by their very nature, new introductions that need market seasoning and feedback. This sets up a conundrum, right? How will they get that market validation until they are truly marketed and put into the hands of early adopters?

When Kenan Systems became a wholly owned subsidiary of Lucent with me still running it the first year and also having been appointed a VP of Bell Labs, I made a radical proposal to the CEO of Lucent and the president of Bell Labs. Since Kenan Systems was wildly profitable (in the first year at Lucent, our 1,000-person company contributed 5 percent of the cash generated by the 135,000-person company that Lucent was at the time), I offered to use the Kenan Systems budget to set up a new entity, the Joint Development and Delivery Center. I would take staff from both Bell Labs (selecting fifty highly innovative team members) and Kenan Systems (selecting fifty with skills in taking innovations to implementation-ready offers). Lucent gave the project a nod, and within six months we had already developed great products that we were marketing at premium prices.

Understandably, the mechanics of sales and marketing at a company are going to be highly visible bones of all-around contention. Everyone can see if the sales team is succeeding, if the marketing is working. Everyone has an opinion on it, and some even think they understand it. (I've never met a marketing genius who claims to understand anything!) Since the stakes are so high, and fevered emotions often run higher, I spent a lot of time looking for a less contentious but equally effective sales and marketing model. The model I ultimately devised was anything but orthodox.

Leads Belong to the Company

Early on, when Kenan Systems had developed a key product, Arbor/BP, for the telecommunications sector, I hired four salespeople using the traditional model with sales plans I wrote for each that included the elements I described earlier. All four had done sales successfully. So, soon they confronted me with handfuls of leads and insisted on converting the leads "their way."

Beyond the leads issue, this sales crew was clearly out there telling prospects whatever it took to make the sale. We had numerous requests for changes to our standard T&Cs, along with customization requests with costs we had to swallow and expedited delivery requests that were wholly unrealistic.

On top of it all, our salespeople became quite possessive of their territories and the leads therein, creating a constant friction that rubbed the team wrong. Soon I found my days spent in near-constant battle with our salespeople.

I began running a noisy exploration in search of a solution to our problems.

How would it work, I wondered, if we separated out lead generation from sales closing? That'd be novel. We could have a marketing team solely responsible for leads. Whoever found the leads or however the leads came, they could go directly to marketing. I could step in and review the leads for their fit with our company's strategies, capacities, culture, resources, and so on. Then the leads that were worth pursuing could be assigned to a salesperson depending on the fit between the prospect and the salesperson.

The idea began to grow on me. There was, to me anyway, an inherent logic to it. So, I assembled our four salespeople and laid out the new plan. Two resigned on the spot, mumbling something about the egghead academic "not getting how sales is done." I sensed a parallel to what the lawyers had told me, and figured I might be on the right track with this new sales strategy. And indeed, there were parallels here to the principle that revenue is by the company, through the company, and for the company. Why shouldn't it apply to leads and resulting sales? So, two corollary principles resulted ...

- Marketing generates leads, the company owns the leads, and the triage team allocates the leads to the sales force.
- Leads are by the company, through the company, for the company.

The two salespeople who didn't storm out that day ended up loving this approach. Turns out they enjoyed and excelled at closing a sale and thought trying to generate the leads was a drag. Here I was offering to take on that process by having a separate team. And I did, by hiring MBAs.

It turns out many MBAs aspire to be executives and know that the path to the C-suite often runs through sales. However, they do not want to take positions as a salesperson. The job we were offering was the dreaded cold-calling part of sales but packaged as marketing, which the MBA hires liked. And they were very good at it. Furthermore, when our prospects expressed a distaste for meeting with "sales types" as they often did, they would gladly respond to an MBA marketing person. And we were able to hire from the top business schools, which made their calling cards even more powerful.

Soon our marketing funnel was filled with leads to be assigned to the right salesperson. The lead triage process helped preserve and reinforce the company's path to streamlined growth. In due time, the sales team became more efficient at closing sales and thus more effective.

This unorthodox model of company-owns-the-leads and the company-assigns-the-leads to each salesperson was successful, to my partial surprise and complete delight. To sum up:

Leads and sales are by the company, through the company, for the company, nicely complementing …

projects by the company are through the company for the company and …

revenue by the company is through the company for the company.

All this may look and feel like disempowered sales and marketing, and it is. Just as with HR, it turns out there is empowerment in disempowerment.

Time has passed and I can still, with so many positive experiences in the can, recommend this unorthodox sales and marketing model—especially when coupled with AAWE hiring and internal talent repurposing.

From Documentation to Sales or Marketing

Earlier, I espoused that documentation specialists should be hired using the AAWE model for the A and W they could bring to the job. I further espoused that liberal arts graduates, with their excellent writing and communication skills, could become great documentation specialists. Both proved to be correct.

So, I noisily explored a less probable idea. Could our documentation specialists who were great at mastering the functional description of all our systems, who could describe our product features and benefits in intimate detail, who ran against stereotypes and could relate to customers magnificently, thusly be great in marketing and even sales positions? Could we repurpose them in that way? Turns out we could, and the numbers proved it. So much so that I also recommend that new hires in sales be required to complete training in documentation.

Crossing the Chasm from Custom Offers to Products

Going from one-off work to repeatable work, that is from the building of custom systems to a product or platform that can serve many, is so critical to a successful LS to LC to RE journey that I'm echoing it here.

More often than not, an LS's offers are one-offs, tailored to the initial customers. Even as the LS evolves into an LC, that could well remain the case despite the team's intense efforts to develop a sustainable product. Many have tried to go from custom to productized. Most have failed.

In discussions earlier, I pointed out two causes of this failure. One is the false notion that the custom crew has often expressed along these lines: "We are bringing in the revenue, and the company is wasting it on this product group that is doomed to fail; we could use all those excellent people who are no longer available to us to generate more revenue, which we certainly can."

These sentiments are usually earnestly held and deeply felt, so they must be met with reasoned, thoughtful responses. They must be handled delicately if the productization crew is to make any progress toward their objectives and the custom crew is to retain their focus. I believe this is best handled by helping all in the company to understand the principle that revenue is by the company, through the company, for the company.

Another massive impediment to transitioning the company from custom to productization is the classical territorial sales model. Under this model, the salespeople are always going to make more money selling the old custom work over the new product line. It cannot be allowed. That's another reason this unorthodox sales model is key to evolving from LS to LC and onward to RE with a big impact.

It has been said, accurately, that in a custom or services-centric company, the assets walk out the door every night and go home to their families. So, the only way to scale up a services-centric company is to hire more people. Not so with productization. This can be exponentially scaled and requires fewer, less-skilled staff to do so.

Another key enabler of the transition over to a product-centric company: excellent documentation.

I took on my company's documentation because I enjoyed it, but also because situational leadership demanded it. My academic training had equipped me to handle documentation much more ably than development—which our crackerjack team handled so brilliantly. So, it became a smart division of labor and a smarter application of another principle—that of comparative advantage. In fortuitous ways, it shaped my approach to leading. I saw how the solid execution of the task of documentation, in turn, gave us more solid offers and a more resilient organizational architecture.

By examining the documentation sets for different custom projects, you can ably identify the common building blocks and move toward products with common cores and flexible shells, i.e., platforms.

Often documentation is viewed as a form of drudgery, and when it is, of course, the output is likely to be sloppy. But if, through predisposition or attitude adjustment or even divine intervention, the LC's handling of documentation can be elevated to a minimum level of proficiency—if a way can be found for that to happen—then the path forward brightens tremendously. And at the risk of appearing brash, I'll go so far as to suggest that *the path from successful* LC *to* RE *runs through documentation.*

TAKEAWAY PRINCIPLES AND VOCABULARY

- Secure enough space for anticipated growth over the short term.
- The layout of offices can be a big factor in creativity and productivity.
- CEO involvement in hiring for support functions is critical.
- Create empowerment by disempowering HR, legal, sales, and marketing.
- Always first try to hire from within with repurposing.
- In performance reviews, use GRRITS (goals, responsibilities, requests, interests, talents, and skills).
- Equip yourself with judicious simplification and ambiguity tolerance.
- Know accounting; know cost accounting even better.
- Pricing should be based on value imparted.
- Write peace contracts when possible.
- Insist on a signed contract before beginning work.
- Documentation is a cornerstone of success.
- Client success, not happiness, should be the foremost objective.
- Use the core-and-shell concept to transition from custom solutions to products.
- Resist the great IP lie at every turn.
- Revenue is for the company, by the company, of the company.

- ⊃ Use bottom-up and top-down thinking but also middle-out thinking.

- ⊃ Marketing generates leads, the company owns the leads, and the triage team allocates the leads to the sales force.

- ⊃ New products require aggressive commission and discount rates, and often a separate sales force.

PART II

CONTINUING AS A LEAN COMPANY

4

INTANGIBLES SUSTAIN THE LEAN COMPANY

Our best writers have helped us evolve culture through their language, for language is the tool for teaching, transmitting, conserving, and practicing cultural beliefs and manners in our lives and for passing them along to the next generation. While the term *culture* can be an ambiguous one, it is arguably the strongest tool in the shed for improving our lives, or as the Dutch historian Johan Huizinga said, "If we are to preserve culture, we must continue to create it."[11]

So, the best way to advance our culture is to generate one description of it after another. Repeated descriptions open our minds to a deeper understanding of all the *intangible qualities* of our culture and, more specifically, the corporate cultures we speak of here.

I believe there is an imprecise set of intangible qualities that cement the foundation of a sustainable company culture and support the construction of something truly amazing. In building my own company, I would try repeatedly to describe these qualities and principles, and in time, they evolved into our own LS to LC to RE lexicon.

---

11   Wikipedia, s.v. "Johan Huizinga," https://en.wikipedia.org/wiki/Johan_Huizinga.

This lexicon became the strongest and sharpest tool in the shed for building a company culture that sustained us right through to that RE.

It can be that tool for you, as well, as long as you continue to evolve the lexicon to reflect the kind of sustainable corporate culture you seek.

The Company Lexicon

I know my editor will flag my insistence on repeating things in varying and differing and repeating ways because, well, editors are taught to be concise. Yet in all my years of teaching, I found that the more times an important idea was framed in a slightly different way, the more power and resonance it held. I even had a lexicon entry for this principle:

Repeat without seemingly repeating.

This repeating notion is more prevalent than many people know, and examples of it are everywhere. For instance, in classical music, a simple tune is presented, then a variation, then another. J. S. Bach's compositions do a masterful job of this. The listener enjoys the repeat seemingly not repeated.

We see it in today's pop music, as well, where there is the body, the chorus, another body, a repeat of the chorus, and so on.

We see it in the spiraling or layering used universally in publishing—from newspapers and magazines to scientific articles. First, there is the title or headline, then a summary or abstract, then the elaborations, and then the summary. All repeating but with more information at each turn of the spiral. (Take note, dear editor.)

In my experience, I found repetition seemingly not repeated to be a powerful adjunct to noisy explorations with a portfolio of offers. Indeed, in talking with prospects, I'd notice them nodding their heads at a regular clip to suggest they were following along, but were they, really? Did they get it, really get it, especially on highly technical subjects? Likely not. So, I would state the point differently. I would keep spiraling or presenting variations while always trying my best to not appear repetitious. It's not always easy!

Company lexicons loaded up with repeating principles that don't come across as repeats can be critical for the development of the culture and structure of an LS and even more so when becoming an LC.

Ownership and Leadership

Let's start the lexicon analysis with ownership. Many founders refer to their company as "my company," and the employees routinely refer to the founder as "our owner" or if there are several, "our owners."

As a former academic, I find these kinds of references not only misleading but genuine impediments to the evolution of an effective company culture.

Think about it this way. A *company*, as the name clearly states, is a group of people that come together to do something. Since these people cannot be owned, neither can a company be owned in the literal sense. The founder has an ownership right in a financial sense, as do the employees. And the forms of these financial ownership interests differ. But nobody owns the company ...

The founder(s) also work for the company.

This notion makes everything simple. Everybody, the founders and employees alike, is united around promoting the interests of the company.

This principle can play out in several ways. For instance, what happens if the founder chooses not to serve as CEO but as CTO instead; is whoever takes the role of CEO now the *owner*? No. But if the founder is viewed as *owning* the company, does the founder then *own* the CEO? Again, no. When the culture is established at the outset on the principle that everybody works for the company, then it becomes much easier to keep clear on all the roles and relationships as they relate to the company's overall best interests.

Another benefit is the ease with which decision-making can be centered around *business* interests rather than *owner* interests. It's a mild version of no one is above the law. No one, not even the founder, is above the company's interests and objectives.

Business objectives, not the owner's interests, are the starting point.

A useful adjunct principle here is situational leadership. Some are exceptional at launching projects but not so good at continuing them. Others are excellent at innovating but not implementing. So, why not have a project developer lead in the early brainstorming and concept stages but then transition leadership to others who can do a better job of enlisting and leading the team that takes it over the line? This would be situational leadership at work.

Practice situational leadership.

Power is sticky and not easily relinquished. However, if leaders make it clear from the outset that transient leadership best serves the company, if that idea is established in the company's culture and incorporated into the LS lexicon with a variety of descriptors, then power transitions will, in the future, be more successful.

Another term for this is aces in places. You always want your talent to be contributing where they are most suited and ready to step into any new situation when needed.

Bringing together these ideas of everyone working for the company and situational leadership, just as with combining hydrogen and oxygen atoms, creates a powerful covalent bond in a company. This bond is then made even stronger by linking it to two other principles of communication flow. To get work done, there has to be a structure and a hierarchy with, at the very least, a team leader and team members. So, orders and directives are issued by the leader—that is natural. But how about information flow? Quite often in companies, the information will flow hierarchically, as well. That, too, feels natural, yet it is far from an effective flow.

Approaches to Decision-Making

In my experience in an LS, setting up a flat network for information flow will result in more effective and adaptive communications. As the company grows into an LC, information flows will inevitably become more layered. Even then, the less layering, the better.

If internal communications are set up in the traditional hierarchical way, no matter how deftly it is done, one standard of practice will develop among team members. This is no secret, this practice. It is so well known that when you ask ten people walking into the elevators of a New York high-rise what's the worst part of the job they otherwise like, they'll say "corporate infighting."

Even when hierarchies are set up with the best of intentions—to marshal the collective talents of the organization into an efficient decision-making machine, it's not long before human nature kicks in and those hydrogen and oxygen atoms are being actively yanked apart.

This yanking is manifest in the way information is filtered, siphoned, amended, appended, disfigured, embellished, and generally distorted by each hand it touches on its way up the hierarchy: one department's pressing interests become another department's immediate problem; or corporate power plays take precedence over larger company objectives. All are well known, yet these hierarchies remain at so many companies.

Why?

First, a little context.

People tend to use the terms *data* and *information* interchangeably, yet they are as different as water and ice. Data is transmitted by a source and only becomes information when received in context. For instance, Neil speaks in Japanese over the phone to Margaret. If Margaret knows Japanese, she can understand and thus receive information. Otherwise, it's all noise to her. Even if Margaret does speak Japanese, what she hears and understands depends on the context, e.g., is it a casual conversation, a business meeting, a technical discussion?

What if we continue with Neil and Margaret, but add Asuka the translator who, it turns out, has her own ulterior motives? What she receives from Neil in Japanese is not literally and faithfully translated but gets tweaked to nuance the messaging that Margaret receives. Even if there are no insidious motives, the translator may have the wrong context. We are all familiar with these kinds of garbled translations. Unless there is a validating mechanism in place, neither Neil nor Margaret will be satisfied with the information flow.

Both of these examples—Neil to Margaret, Neil through Asuka to Margaret—are illustrative of what happens in hierarchical communication networks.

Setting up flat communication pathways can mitigate all these "human nature" problems. It doesn't end them; it just combats them. In these flat pathways, the data is transmitted directly from the source to the ultimate end user. It comes as close as possible to being unaltered data and thus better information in the hands of the ultimate end user.

Many times in the day-to-day of business life, the timely receipt of source data is just not possible because this end user is too busy. It's a legitimate concern. You may want to see all the source data, but as the company grows, there just are not enough hours in the day. That is why hierarchies naturally evolve—to protect the schedules of each person on up the ladder. That's why admins are put in place—to watch the gate and not allow the boss to get overwhelmed with a thousand daily requests—all of them seemingly important.

Indeed, early on at Kenan Systems, we were growing so fast that our original lines of authority were becoming muddled, and I thought hierarchies might help us manage the workload more efficiently. I allowed the company to begin layering. And then almost instantly regretted it … as the company's information flows began distorting predictably.

So I decided to practice the idea of interruptibility. My administrative assistant would sit a safe distance from my office door. That door would be always open except when I was in a confidential meeting or on a call. I let everyone on the team know that I was free to be interrupted if they had a question or data to share or anything that might benefit from a rapid response.

To attach an internal value to the kinds of questions worth interrupting for, I set a limit of five per person per day. Rarely were there five, but two to three was common. And it worked.

In turn, of course, I reserved the right to interrupt my colleagues without notice—if their door was open or if that invisible door that's attached to every cubicle appeared to be open. Again, it worked by the key metric we were judging ourselves by—efficiency of communications flows.

All these practices—flattened communications, preservation of source data, and judicious interruption of colleagues—added up to vastly improved team connectivity in an equation we expressed quite simply as *data > information > better decision-making*.

Perhaps one of the most unyielding obstacles to effective decision-making is the problem created by combinatorial complexity.

Dealing with Combinatorial Complexity

Turning data into information in tight decision time frames can be challenging, or not. In many situations, our brains do it so well we are unaware of the underlying complexities of this data-to-information conversion. In walking, for example, we have no problem assessing the terrain data, having a good mental map of our body, and then taking our steps just in time. That is because of learned behavior, and we are reminded of it when trying to teach a child or a robot to walk. But quite often, these conversions are intrinsically complex.

Take the Brooklyn Bridge. Given the number of cars passing it, what is the load on a particular beam of the bridge? Converting data into information in this situation requires solving rather intense calculus equations.

There is another kind of complexity that appears straightforward but is quite challenging for decision-making. I speak of combinatorial complexity.

It becomes relevant the minute you hear somebody utter that common refrain, "I need all the data before I can make the decision." Let's look at what this decision-maker is actually asking for, and what it means, using an example we see all around us—a display of lights.

Let's say we have a display panel of twenty by twenty light bulbs, which, by doing the math, we know adds up to four hundred bulbs. This is actually a primitive display panel by today's stadium jumbotron standards. But staying focused on our little panel, let's ask a question: How many unique patterns could be displayed in it?

If it were just one bulb, we could have two patterns, right?

If it were two bulbs, we could have two by two; with three, we could have two by two by two and so forth on up to four hundred bulbs, which is expressed as 2^{400} (2 to the power of 400) or about 10^{120}. A big number.

Let's assume that for a particular decision, we want to find the best pattern (according to some criterion among the 10^{120} patterns we can generate with our primitive array). How long would it take us?

We'd need to examine every possible pattern since the best pattern may be the one we check last. Now assume we have a superfast computer helping us. How long do you think it would take to find the best light pattern in just those four hundred bulbs?

When I've put this question to my students, the answers have come back: two seconds, one minute, a half hour. With AI, some will now say, it can be done in three hundred milliseconds.

Suppose our computer is superfast and can crunch through ten billion or 10^10 patterns a second. The time for the complete examination would be 10^120 patterns divided by 10^10 patterns per second or 10^110 seconds. Sounds like a lot of seconds. It is. It's longer than the presumed age of the universe ... which is plus or minus fourteen billion years.

What if we assume an utterly impossible setup: Every elementary particle in the universe—all the electrons, photons, neutrons, bosons, etc.—is in fact a little supercomputer. And we daisy-chain all these supercomputers together to solve the problem. There are an estimated 10^70 elementary particles in the known universe, and so, yes, 10^70 supercomputers are put to the task. Here's how this equation works out:

10^70 supercomputers x 10^10 patterns per second for 10^120 patterns = 10^40 seconds > the age of the universe

All these supercomputers could not find the best pattern in a humble display device of twenty by twenty bulbs even if the task started at the Big Bang. That's how unfathomable combinatorial complexity can be. And here is the novice executive at a company saying he wants to wait for all the information to come in before he acts!

Here is an actual context: matching staff members to projects to be undertaken. This is exacerbated when both the staff size and the projects grow and even more so when a project is divided into subprojects.

Even with only a handful of employees, how do you optimally match skills and interests with the requirements of the project? It's a common decision-making issue. During WWII, this was one of the combinatorial complexities that the armed forces faced in determining how best to mobilize troops across far-flung arenas of battle.

These kinds of issues led to a discipline known as operations research. More aptly, it was a multidiscipline because it brought together experts from many fields to find solutions to seemingly intractable matters. After WWII, the field survived and expanded into management science. Today, the algorithms developed postwar are used by companies such as Amazon, UPS, and USPS to determine the optimal navigation routes for their delivery trucks.

The Value of Judicious Simplification

How to handle this inherent cruelty in combinatorial complexity? With judicious simplification.

People have been judiciously simplifying ever since the choice was either face the mastodon alone or get some guys together. Our emotions are natural simplifiers, and we call it "gut feel." Faced with mounds of data, we intuitively reach a conclusion between I like it, I reject it, or I'll think about it.

Sometimes these intuitions are codified into rules of thumb and called heuristics to lend an air of legitimacy. There's even a branch of management science called heuristic programming.

There's also a more formal and, in my view, more robust approach to simplification: statistical sampling. For instance, to take the pulse of the electorate, you can canvass all the voters. Slow, expensive. Or you can randomly select one thousand voters to poll and get a fairly reliable assessment. Pollsters do this very thing. In knowing how to set up the math, they can come meaningfully close to the accuracy of full canvassing.

Another approach is akin to tree pruning. You convert the decision space into a tree of alternatives with each branch dependent on the next lower branch in deciding which ones merit examination. Again, using gut feel or heuristics, one can lop off huge branches for simplification. Alas, sometimes the branches that have the fruit we are seeking are lopped off. Hence the term *judicious*. The art of good decision-making improves with better heuristics in deciding what to cut. No cuts, we face combinatorial complexity. Wrong cuts, we end up with a fruitless data-to-information conversion and decision-making.

A formal approach to this is Bayesian analysis. Starting with an initial belief (prior probability), it combines this with new data (likelihood) to produce an updated belief (posterior probability). This method allows for a dynamic and flexible statistical inference that incorporates prior knowledge and new information.

Another powerful statistical tool is regression analysis and, beyond that, multivariate analysis. There are many more, these days enhanced by AI.

Our goal is not to venture into these analytical tools but to be clear that a full plate of information cannot be available in every decision-making situation and, in fact, ideally *should not be.* The art and science of moving ahead with partial information should become the mindset of every team member and be incorporated into the company lexicon.

This said, I know from experience that the very idea of working with only "partial information" makes some people, especially the technically trained, uncomfortable. That is why I digressed into the twenty-by-twenty display example: to make the point that in simplifying, the perfect is the enemy of the good. (Very different from earlier where in a hiring situation, the good is the enemy of the excellent!) Let's layer on another level of complexity: ambiguity.

With the light bulbs, there is no ambiguity in the state: The bulb is either on or off. But in making decisions about employees and their skill sets, there is no end to the ambiguities that creep in. So, the decision maker must *develop a high tolerance for ambiguity.*

Knowing that it is impossible to disambiguate many of the factors we face in making decisions, knowing this and accepting it as well, then it becomes easier to make a decision with a reasonable level of certainty and clarity and then move on, content with the decision.

Presocialization of Decisions

At this point, we have flattened communications that afford many-to-many access in the organization, we have interruptibility embedded into the daily interactivity of the team, we have enriched decision-making through ambiguity tolerance, and now we add what I call decisions after socialization.

This can be described in many ways: staging a decision, trial ballooning it, priming the pump, or having a "hearing" on it, which we see so often in government. Making key decisions only after first involving the broader staff in a flattened interruptible environment results in higher-quality decisions that everyone on the team will more willingly support—because in fact, they already have.

Now this is not some Pollyannaish whimsy I'm engaged in. I fully recognize that companies are not technically democracies on some one-employee-one-vote model. But the ideal of trying your utmost to incorporate or socialize as many of the team's ideas and inputs into a decision as possible is a good one.

That's because the acceptance of the decision is, in effect, being primed by the very people who will be most impacted by it and carrying it out. In a real sense, the extra time that this socialization requires will more than make up for the shortened time to acceptance and enthusiastic execution. And it is a good complement to situational leadership, as well.

One way of operationalizing socialized decision-making is management by walking around. This practice of walking the halls makes interruptibility easier for everyone and works to obtain data directly from the sources, or at least closer to the sources.

Making better and better-accepted decisions is obviously a good thing, but the real rub is usually which decisions need making in which order. This leads to the creation of a decision agenda. What goes onto this agenda is usually more important than how it's handled. And again, the practice of socialization can help—not only in the development of the decision agenda, but also in its iterations moving forward.

So, it is a good practice early on to *embed in the culture the preparation of decision agendas*, which are then discussed, revised, and finalized (socialized).

Care to Validating Assumptions

We make decisions based on … what? On the pure data we have, sure. But also on all the assumptions, hypotheses, speculations, and conjectures running around in our brains. The human mind is a remarkable conjecture generator. We can also convince ourselves that these conjectures are truly incontrovertible truths. Knowing this about ourselves, it is critical that we at least label them all as assumptions. This gives us a jumping-off point. It helps us avoid making erroneous decisions almost every time if we begin with our assumptions and then set out to validate them.

Vignettes of this assumption-making process in the corporate world include the following:

"That company will never buy our products," Alice says. "Why even try?"

"How do you know this, Alice?"

"Well, Joe from that company said so."

"You're making two huge assumptions here, that Joe represents the whole company, and that Joe won't change his mind."

"I know what the client will say," Chester, the head salesman, tells the boss.

"Really? Do you know what I am going to say next?"

"Uh, no?"

"Right, you and I have known each other for quite some time, and we work together. You can't even guess what I'm going to say next? Yet you are confident you know what the client will say?"

"Yes, that is a good idea, but surely someone out there has already thought about it and made it into a product."

"Really, can you be any more defeatist?"

Now consider how easily these assumptions can be validated when socialized up and down the halls of the company. All the more so when repetition without repeating is used, like holding the facets of a diamond at different angles to bring a new light on things. Social scientists practice this in questionnaires.

They ask the same question multiple times but each time with a variation, gaining true insights into the individual's thought patterns. Many business analysts practice this principle as well by constructing a variety of models into which they embed a variety of scenarios to gauge potentially different outcomes in the marketplace.

Earlier we talked about source data as if it stands on the pantheon of good decision-making fodder, free of assumptions. But, of course, that's not the case. Assumptions are embedded into everything we touch to some degree. Even the most robust mathematical formulas are based on assumptions.

It is in the validating of assumptions that great decisions are made.

On the Timing of Decisions

I could bring even more perspectives to the decision-making process, but then we begin to risk paralysis by analysis, narrowing the window you have on actually making a decision and then implementing it. So, yes, the time that's devoted to decision-making must be carefully governed. Not too soon, not too late. Not too fast, not too slow.

Operationally what does that mean? As usual, it all depends on the context. However, there is a broad concept that applies here: synchrony. I will not go deep into the concept but rather illustrate it with the cup of coffee I used to carry from classroom to classroom at MIT in a time when professors still wrote on chalkboards. Since chalk dust would get into my mouth, I'd use a sip of coffee to wash it down and keep the throat moist. As I walked across the corridors, the janitors would eye me warily, lest I spill the coffee. I never did, though, and I thank timely decision-making. Meaning?

I never looked at the coffee cup. If you look at the coffee swishing away as you move, the natural reaction is to move your arm in the opposite direction, which pushes little coffee waves in the opposite direction but also amplifies them. Pretty soon the coffee is slushing around and, of course, it spills over.

It's the timing and frequency of intervention decisions that trigger the very outcome we aim to prevent. Our eyes see and our minds react much faster than the coffee waves and the result is … amplification. Response and reaction are out of sync. I would instead let my arm do the sensing. The response time of the arm is more in tune with the reaction time of the coffee waves.

This coffee story has valuable analogs, I believe. For instance, a retail company's inventory levels might be running low. The company buyer, fearing the item will be out of stock, puts in an order. Alas, due to lag times, the item is sold out at the wholesaler. In a panic, the buyer puts in another order or has the first one expedited. Meantime, demand declines because shoppers assume the item will be out of stock for a while, or they switch to a substitute. The order arrives, but now there is a surplus with less demand, as well. So, now the decision is an overstock sale. Demand can now overshoot, leading to another out-of-stock situation, new orders being placed, etc.

In such a situation, it can again be helpful to socialize across the company to get input and insights. Perhaps the increase in demand a company is seeing is a direct result, known only to Thomas in marketing, that a cheaper competitor is currently out of stock on the item. Knowing that would argue for taking a patient approach to the new customer demand since it could go away once the competitor stocks up.

From Less Comes More

By its very nature, an LS is always tight on money, space, staff, capacity, skills—most everything, really! While some would view these as obstacles, they also can be sources of strength. The lexicon entry here is *from less can come more.*

Paradoxical as it may at first sound, our human imagination, ingenuity, and capacity to innovate can all three be stimulated in scarcity, shortages, and hardship. That's why I highly recommend that the notion of doing more with less be instilled in the company's culture early on. There are many variations of this principle such as minimalism, frugality, parsimony, and Yankee ingenuity.

We see it in some of America's finest companies. This minimalist mindset is said to have been deeply embedded in Apple's early culture and partly responsible for some superb engineering.

Academia can be a great practitioner of less is more. A department of a branch of engineering might be just ten or twenty people.

This is the case at MIT School of Engineering, which has been rated number one in engineering almost every year for the past fifty years. Overall, MIT's five schools (Engineering, Architecture, Science, Humanities and Social Sciences, and Management) have been ranked in the top five in the same period. The school has more than eighty Nobel laureates. Companies spawned from MIT generate more than $2 trillion in revenue every year, more than the economy of India. Yet, MIT had only one thousand faculty members in 1963, and it's still the same in 2023. So, the school has clearly accomplished more—a lot more—with less.

MIT is not unique—not in this sense, anyway. Most universities practice the idea of limiting growth to expand the output.

Teach and Learn, Learn and Teach

One of the great practices of academia, and the thing that makes higher education so powerful, is that the professors are compelled to learn and teach, and in return teach and learn. I strongly believe every LS should make this a cornerstone principle. It's not just an attitude or orientation, but something to put into practice every day.

Academics teach in front of their students, deliver talks at conferences, write papers, referee papers, publish textbooks, and have to read and read and read. They are cast in a never-ending cycle of teaching and learning and relearning and teaching. By contrast in many companies, knowledge is often quickly compartmentalized and unavailable except to those in the immediate purview. Worse, it goes stale because it is so infrequently shared. There is insufficient validating, refreshing, and enriching of this company knowledge. And when it happens, it becomes a sizable obstacle to success.

This key *teach and learn, learn and teach* principle is another great complement to situational leadership. Think about it.

If information is being compartmentalized and not widely shared outside the immediate purview, then what happens when it becomes necessary to shift an employee from one area of the company to another? That employee is plenty talented in one department, no doubt, but comes into the new department with a serious information deficit—a serious disadvantage.

But with teach and learn, learn and teach in action, a small team is in the position to accomplish a great deal more than the gross numbers suggest.

Here's another angle on this idea. We may think that we are the same person day in and day out, an hour in and hour out, and that society assumes as much, as well. But in truth, we are many people in one. These aspects of ourselves are manifested in different contexts. At work, we might be a subordinate and a conformist. As the president of the canoe club, we are a leader and an explorer. As a parent, an educator and a nurturer. And so on. So, why not leverage these multiple personalities we have in a workplace context?

Management, Sure, but How Much?

At around ten people or so, the startup begins to feel like the real deal. This is often when combinatorial complexity starts gathering steam with managerial tasks multiplying. The temptation is to add to management staff to meet the growing project load. As this happens, the *do more with less* principle should be revisited because it applies as effectively to management activities as to technical ones.

A good approach at this point is to incorporate a qualitative metric to assess a manager's ideal workload allocation. For example, managerial hours should not exceed XX percent of total work hours (management and technical combined). In my experience, 5 percent to 10 percent is a good range.

A note on the use of these kinds of qualitative metrics. When attaching metrics to complex activities, it's important to keep them general. Otherwise, managers may get distracted by the pressure to hit a specific target figure. For instance, instead of having a hard-and-fast rule such as 5 percent, better to say around 5 percent.

There is a good example of this from academia. Exam scores are often quantitative (95, 87, 62), but the grades are qualitative (A, B, D). Some graders can't bring themselves to be that vague, and they succumb to giving an A- because they struggle at the margins. If the range for B is 80 to 89, and exam scores average 89 for a student, is that a B? Well, so is an 80. Isn't that unfair? So, why not A-? It is a slippery slope. Quantification is never easy.

In this era, there is another reason to keep management lean. Generative AI (or what I prefer to call IE, for intelligence extensions) can act as our assistants in so many ways. The current thinking seems to be that IE will consolidate many white-collar positions, including management ones. But if those positions are already lean, instead of eliminating positions, the company can more easily adopt and deploy IEs.

As an example, an earlier form of IE, word processing, eliminated huge numbers of secretarial positions. Shortly after that, spreadsheets on computers eliminated huge numbers of bookkeepers and subsequently, midlevel management positions. Euphemistically, the massive downsizing of midlevel managers was called "rightsizing." We are now facing an even bigger downsizing (or rightsizing?) across the white-collar workforce of many professions because of the rapid emergence of IEs. So, for a startup that's running lean and aims to remain lean, why not be the *right size* at the early stages and keep that culture going?

In a tightly and parsimoniously run startup, the CEO is under tremendous pressure from day one. Pressure that comes from there being too much to do, generally. To manage this situation—to drink from the fire hose every day, as they say—I believe the smartest practice is to encourage interruptibility and get up from the desk every half hour whenever possible to walk the halls, check in at people's desks, interrupt them, sometimes disrupt them, and encourage the same back from them. This enabling of decentralized flat communications can leverage the company's best source data, turning it at once into valuable information that advances the company forward faster.

Situational leadership again comes into play in reducing the pressure on management. In this sense, situational leadership is akin to delegation, only it's not as static. It is innately dynamic and thus organically powerful.

Power, What of It?

In every situation, the raw stuff of *power* tends to increase in concentration as it rises up the hierarchy. It happens in companies too. As a startup grows and a hierarchy inevitably emerges, power concentrates on top. That concentrating action soon begins to feel quite disempowering for those down the ladder in a still-small and otherwise intimate organization where there had been a feeling of egalitarianism. From this, very human problems begin and dysfunction rears its ugly head—often for the first time.

There is no surprise in these observations. They are well known, right?

Power is a corruptive and addictive force. When power concentrates in an LS, many of the principles espoused in this book become difficult to practice. Gone is situational leadership—power is sticky and it doesn't let go. Gone is interruptibility—who dares interrupt a more powerful superior? Gone are unfiltered information flows—

folks down the ladder try to package the news in the ways power likes, to curry favor.

More importantly, if power is concentrated at a few nodes in the company, and other nodes are relatively disempowered and that remains so, the company loses its ability to innovate. Let me summarize this from two perspectives:

- The concentration of power in a few nodes disempowers other nodes.
- Disempowerment suppresses innovation and initiative.

It's worth noting that we are here speaking of the power dynamics of the company in general. For as you may be thinking, I've spent a good portion of this book talking about why I disempowered HR, legal, accounting, and other support functions at Kenan Systems.

Keyword: support functions.

Those in supporting roles can be disempowered to become better empowered, but for the company in general, the power dynamic must work differently to bring out the natural innovation and initiative in each team member.

In the classroom, I used to pontificate that a highly empowered CEO can be a menace to the company and its customers —and if the company was a highly impactful one, a menace to society itself.

A manifestation of power concentration at the top is when the CEO begins to view the company as his or her company and treats it like personal property. Conversations such as "You work for me" and "I own the work product" and even "It is my revenue, my profits, and I can do whatever I like with it" become commonplace. It sounds almost melodramatic as I write it here, like something out of an episode of *Succession* on TV, yet this hubris in CEOs is rather common. It is also dangerous.

How Power Concentrates

At the outset, power is naturally concentrated at the top, there being only a couple of team members. Then it is dispersed, hopefully in businesswise ways. Then soon enough individuals in the company seek to grab for power—whether with intention or as a byproduct of their actions.

There are many ways in which a company, often inadvertently, causes a power concentration. One is to make an individual indispensable. The reward for doing an outstanding job is to get more of the same kind of work. In time, these "indispensables" acquire so much competence and become such a hub that they are, in fact, power centers unto themselves.

Some individuals will plot to become indispensable by being the go-tos. They'll go around collecting information and offering their services, and step by step, they are the one to go to. They will learn but not necessarily teach; they will offer solutions but not "show their work." The more that happens, the more colleagues seek them out, and soon they are powerful nodes, even viewed as indispensable.

Some are skilled at acquiring power by association. They deliberately pop into the picture close to the power nodes, hobnobbing with them so others in the organization think they have power or at least influence. This becomes a self-engendering path to power because then others seek them out—thinking them powerful—and thus they become so.

These individuals often practice a two-way association with both power nodes and with staff. Their position of power is thus reinforced from above and below, from the more powerful who make the key decisions and the less powerful who carry out those decisions.

There are dangers to allowing these practices to continue. The most immediate of many dangers is that these individuals will become viewed as spokespeople by top management and might say to the staff, "Senior management wants x, y, z." At the same time, since top management views them as closely associated with the staff, they might tell the management, "The staff wants a, b, c." It's an effective way to manipulate.

And it is best nipped in the bud by interruptibility. If the CEO is going around the office interrupting and checking in at random desks, it can short-circuit and disrupt any budding mini-networks of manipulative power concentration.

Then there are the heroes—either self-declared or designated by the team. Take the person who invented the product that the company now hangs its hat on. Is this inventor the hero in this situation?

Many would say yes; I would say no. Many others were probably involved in that invention, and the company or its investors actually capitalized it. The inventor is not the hero; the entire team involved with the product is the hero. I learned this lesson in transitioning from academia to industry.

I had invented a new product, I owned the patent on it, I was considered the hero in this story, and I'll admit to being quite proud of my product. But then I realized that the real heroism is in the implementation. As they say, ideas are cheap; the execution is the hard part. Yet it's rare in business for the operations people, the marketers, or salespeople to be put on pedestals.

They should be.

And recognizing this is part of the struggle a CEO faces in properly diffusing power so the company itself is always the hero. Yes, the CEO must *know the ways of diffusing power.*

Power is dangerous, corruptive, addictive, yet essential to the functioning of any ecosystem or organization. So, the task is not to eliminate power, of course, but to dynamically balance its locus, strength, and value.

This diffusing of power makes a company more resilient and adaptive. It can also make the company more innovative—potentially much more so, in fact. That's because it builds competencies in at multiple levels of the organization, and the individuals at each of these levels are empowered with situational leadership to identify opportunities and find solutions to client needs in real time.

From this can emerge all kinds of innovations in all their manifestations—additions to a client order, deviations from a wayward path of research, modifications to a module that allow it to be cross-sold—and on and on the examples go of innovations driven by competencies distributed across the organization.

Mitigating Hero Worship

So, yes, I've always discouraged hero worship and even fired heroes (or at least playfully pretended to). When people are put on a pedestal, they can only fall. When they are instead recognized for an outstanding contribution to the team effort, everyone rises.

I'm also wary of people who finagle a position of being the go-to person, so I seek to break their hold. It's not easy—especially with the super well-intentioned—but it is essential. Foremost, I caution staff not to become indispensable because if they do, then forget about vacations, and bring in a cot, you're on call 24/7, and our company is no better off for it. Better that competencies are distributed upward and sideways in the organization so that everybody is dispensable and a value-add to the organization.

Some companies rotate their people on regular schedules, such as for staff development and to deal with power concentration. Banks do it to combat internal fraud. When power meets money, people get tempted. We've all heard the stories. Better to keep rotating people or to send key resource-controlling staffers off on long vacations with replacement teams temporarily stepping in to ensure that company standards are being upheld.

Korean companies are well known for rotating top-tier leaders. Often annually, the top management of these companies enters a cocoon and reemerges from their chrysalis with new portfolios and an all-new management configuration.

However rotations are handled, whether periodic or ad hoc, they offer companies a big advantage. They enable teach and learn, learn and teach in their organizations, and there is arguably no more powerful driver of business success.

Checking and Balancing

Whenever power and resources are in proximity, there must be checkers and balancers looking over shoulders. A good example of this is the separation of accounting and treasury activities, with each office granted review authority over the other.

These oversight activities would seem to suggest that trust is not implicit, and shouldn't a company trust its employees? Yes, but trust without verification is like a fish without water. So, the question of trust is simplified greatly when it is considered always within the context of verification.

In embedding these ideas into the company culture, it becomes easy to say, "Let's both count the money." Who can object to that? It combines trust with good business practice.

So, as the LS becomes an LC and offices are added, a good principle is to establish an arm's length separation between the functional groups such as legal, accounting, finance, and the CEO. That mitigates many temptations.

In the latest ventures I am involved in, even though I am the sole shareholder, from the onset, I established an arm's-length relationship with the controller, the head of contracting, and legal. I instructed them all to follow best practices, knowing that they understood those practices well.

I told them that if I ever asked for anything that did not conform to best practices, they should speak up. If later I found out that they did not do so, I would expect their letter of resignation.

To this day, I do not issue a check or initiate a wire transfer by myself. There is always a second party. Many times, the controller and I will have discussions about how to treat an expense or revenue item, sometimes getting into the weeds on it. If the controller does not agree with me, it is my burden to convince her with references to the relevant literature.

The CEO Checked

Back to my classroom pontifications about an unchecked and unbridled CEO being a real menace to the company. If this idea resonates with you, the next question is: Who in their right mind is going to try checking the most powerful person in the company? Nobody, usually … except the board. In many states in the US, if there are multiple shareholders, then a board is mandated. If venture capitalists are involved, they, too, insist on a board and often sit on it.

At the LS level, it is not easy to assemble a worthwhile board. More likely a board formed at the outset will be a couple of friends who get paid a few bucks to attend quarterly meetings and offer little in the way of useful guidance. A good option in the beginning then, up until when the LS reaches ten or more employees, is to assemble an advisory board.

Should one or more of the key employees be on the advisory board? This is a highly context-dependent question, and one worth careful consideration.

Whether there is a board or not, there are two company functions that require checks and balances: finance/accounting and legal.

We already talked about how finance and accounting should be provisioned to be mutually monitored. Even more important is how the CEO relates to accounting, treasury, and legal once the LS has become an LC and the CEO cannot be intimately involved in each function any longer and the issues and sums are larger.

In the rush of things, it can be quite tempting for CEOs to engage in what we euphemistically call questionable practices regarding money matters. So, the simplest approach is to not trust oneself.

A man is asked, Are you honest? He answers he does not know, as he has not been tested for his honesty. A truly honest and wise answer. A sure way to deal with temptation is to assume nobody is above it.

The Yin and Yang of Power

Ancient wisdom held that the interaction of opposing forces formed a stronger, more harmonious balance, what became known as the yin and yang of life. This wisdom extended to the exercise of power … though it was then and is now a difficult bit of wisdom to apply in the real-world contexts we find ourselves in.

For instance, I've been making the argument here that power should be diffused with checks and balances put in place for a more vibrant and innovative culture. However, there are downsides to distributed power.

Sometimes, synchronous implementation requires a clear chain of command and strict nonquestioning follow-through. Sometimes when a rapid and targeted action is warranted, power has to step up. In short, sometimes it's best to have a single cook in the kitchen.

A classic experiment conducted by MIT's Alex Bavelas in the 1950s illustrated this yin and yang of innovation and implementation. Group A was organized into a round ring formation and people could only communicate with the person on either side of them. Group B was organized into a hub and spokes formation and could only communicate with the hub, not with neighbors.

Each group was presented with a problem and asked to come up with solutions and choose one for implementation. The round-ring-formation group came up with a rich set of solutions (more innovative) but took much longer to settle on the one to be implemented (slower to decide). The hub-and-spokes group generated fewer solutions but was faster to implement them. So, which organizational design proved better?

Well, it's situationally dependent, of course. If a fire bursts out in the company's computer room, there's no time to engage in neighborly consults about what to do. Action is of the essence by the people (the ring) on the scene. However, if a company's product lines are threatened by emerging competition, having several or even many centers of power and initiative in the company (hub and spokes) might lead to a better survival because time is of the essence.

Power and Personality

Then there is power and personality. This was classically illustrated by yet another MIT professor, Douglas McGregor, in what he called Theory X and Theory Y. McGregor's X managers were the hard-minded authoritarians who believed employees had to be tightly controlled lest they go off the rails. Y managers were the opposite, soft-hearted consultative types who believed that empowering subordinates resulted in better consensus-based decisions.

Two contrasting modes of employee motivation, so which won out?

McGregor suggested, and I concur, that it's best to have both styles in the company, again in the yin and yang sense. Now let's tie this X and Y notion to situational leadership. Brainstorming a new product offering can definitely benefit from groupthink and Y-type leadership. But when the project finally goes into R&D, a leader with more X in her might be more effective. And when that product then goes into production, there has to be a chain of command all the way. Not good for someone on the assembly line to take the initiative and install the tire on the car in his clever new way (though sending notes back through the Y would be valuable, so Y benefits from a little flexibility).

Through the yin and yang, the ring and hub-and-spokes, the X and Y, we can see how *both authoritarian and consultative managers are needed* in the company, for they can complement each other well.

Face of the Company

With the rise of the internet and social media, companies have come under tremendous pressure to have a "face" for an unsparing public to judge. This is quite a recent phenomenon. In the last century, the company's face, usually the CEO, was rarely a recognized public figure. Now the public, through a billion hypercritical media lenses, is incessantly demanding that the CEO deliver on a dramatic plot line.

Whether this emerging societal phenomenon is good or bad depends, I suspect, on your view of how much power a CEO should have.

It's certainly true that if a CEO is unchecked by a board or appropriate checks and balances, the temptation is great to grab for more power and stumble into a crisis or scandal, in turn becoming more authoritarian and secretive, and in the worst-case becoming despotic and arbitrary, wielding power for power's sake.

Regrettably, our current era is not lacking in these very CEOs who, left unchecked, become a menace to their company and customers, and to society itself. Even more regrettably, when the CEO, as the face of the company, becomes a public hero and in time is believed indispensable, it is much harder for the board to countermand her. Or it can go the other way. The CEO is so powerful she can populate the board with her loyalists; then even a shareholder revolt won't help, and the business risks stagnating and eventually failing.

We've spoken about this concern of an unchecked CEO twice now because it is a very real, and in my view, underappreciated concern. It is the reason to have a full grasp of the key principles—checks and balances, power sharing, situational leadership—and to embed these principles into the company's culture from day one.

The Modern Phenomenon of Immediacy

Indulge me in revisiting a time when the internet, email, and texts didn't exist. When a phone call came in to a manager, typically it was received by a secretary, noted on a pink pad, torn off, and skewered to a spindle (occasionally a phone number including an 8 became a 0, but we persevered). The manager would grab the messages and read them at periodic hours, ask the secretary to return some of the calls, or schedule a call for the manager to make.

All this took days. If messages arrived by the postal service, the secretary would sort through them, process them into piles, placing the most urgent appearing on the manager's desk. If a manager needed to respond, he called in the secretary and dictated a letter to then be typed up, proofed, often retyped, reproofed, and put into a mail pouch. Someone from the mailroom would arrive, usually late in the day, to pick up the pouches and see to it that their contents were all delivered to the post office. The turnaround time for that single letter could be one to two weeks. If speed was of the essence, couriers were used. In that entire process, did the manager type a single word? No way. That was for secretaries.

Now, the old phone call is endangered, and in its place, text messages fly on to the manager's cellphone at all hours. He'd better answer quickly. Letters are now emails, long ones, often with longer attachments. Any delay in replying and another email follows, or worse, a text: *Sent you an email ... Did you receive ... Await your answer*. Not an answer from your secretary. From you.

Then there's the latest wrinkle. Managers are sending their direct reports one-word text messages just saying *heh* ... that's it. That's beginning to pass for management with harried millennials.

All's to say, for better and worse, it appears, response times have become incredibly short. Remember the example of carrying a mug of coffee around the office? The quicker you are to prevent a spill, the more likely your coffee spills because your response time and the coffee's natural slushing frequency don't match. Being quick to the trigger works against you. In this new world of complex decision-making amid near-instantaneous communications, it is the same.

So, I was amazed at a piece of advice I saw recently. Before proceeding with a decision, the advice went, take a deep breath and wait at least five seconds. Five seconds only. In the old days, the slow pace of communications alone forced waits of days if not weeks before decisions.

We've cycled through this idea from the "takes weeks" to the "takes seconds" era because there is a very real impact on a company's leadership. In slouching toward immediacy, as we have, a leader loses the window to properly socialize an idea, or convene the troops for a brainstorming session, or even run it by a spouse over breakfast. Just no time. Have to act. Must deal with it now.

Could there be a situation more rife with risk?

So, what is the antidote? Taking those five seconds, at least those five, to get a handle on the risks at hand is a start. Not a good start, but a start.

An old joke puts this notion of immediacy into perspective. If a manager takes off for a two-week vacation totally unplugged, and in her absence the company is fine, she's a good manager. If she can stretch that to four weeks and all is fine, she is an excellent manager. If she is gone six weeks and all is fine, she is redundant, no need to come back.

Finding the Balance

This new immediacy mode, especially when coupled with social media–driven amplification of even our smallest failures, has blurred the old separation between company life and personal life. Going back to that distant era, when employees went home, they fully went home. I heard once how John Kennedy was home in Massachusetts late one evening and not feeling well. His assistant decided to call a doctor. The doctor's wife did pick up but admonished the future president for calling after hours.

Nowadays, of course, people and their phones are attached at the hip around the clock with texts and transcribed voicemails incoming nonstop. If a person arises in the middle of the night, email and messages are checked. So, does work mode ever really stop? For most, no.

A corny story. Consultants, lawyers, and similar type professionals keep logs of their time for billing. A consultant, his phone always at hand, decides that the time he spends checking email and texts is billable according to a special formula he has devised. The billing department notices that his billable hours are topping twenty per day. When asked how he manages this feat, he explains that he checks his phone tirelessly almost every waking hour, and that's billable. Plus, since his mind is so saturated with work, he now dreams about his projects, and has decided to include those hours as billable too. Hence, twenty hours!

At Kenan Systems, even before smartphones came along, I would work around the clock but make a point of coming home. In one of my client visits after just receiving a huge contract from them, I went around the client offices thanking the relevant people and wishing them a happy weekend, thinking it was Friday. Only later at the airport did I realize with some embarrassment and disbelief that it was not Friday, but Wednesday. What must the client's staff have thought of me? That I take off on Wednesdays for really long weekends?

That same night, I was met with another surprise. When I arrived home late, my wife confronted me and insisted that my priorities were all wrong. I hadn't eaten dinner with my family in months. I tried to prove otherwise, pulling out my logbook, which unfortunately showed that yes, I may have moved heaven and earth if not the galaxies to make it home, but it was almost always very, very late. Sure, the children would stay up late to see me, and we'd have late-night snacks—but not exactly a proper family dinner.

That night, I resolved to change, and swiftly. Next day at the office, I told the team that henceforth, we would try for balance in our lives. No more working beyond eight at night, and no weekends. Travel would be with the willing consent of the staff. I would not call after hours or weekends. And I wouldn't take calls, except in emergencies. We would create a dynamic balance of work and personal life.

How did that work out for us?

After the initial disbelief and figuring I was just joking around, the team began embracing the soft edict. Embracing it enthusiastically, to my delight. Yet I kept observing that when the intense pressure of project deadlines hit, managers were quick to make exceptions. Absent a firm edict, it appeared the company would revert to working around the clock.

So, another team meeting—this time at a company party with the spouses present. There I appointed myself to the newly created position of balance police and asked all present to notify me directly whenever they thought the "balance" was being breached.

As for the results of that? Well, mixed.

More than once, a project manager blamed me for ruining his delivery schedule. And on one occasion, a big client in London wanted our company lead to fly from our Denver office to London right away, but the lead had family plans locked in for that weekend and declined. When I informed the client of this, I could hear a fist slamming a desk. But that is how a better overall company culture was enforced.

It is practically essential for the CEO to be the balance enforcer. Otherwise, the best of clients and managers will make work a priority.

Balance Creates Healthy Slack

While we didn't see any quantifiable benefits from the new balance edicts right away, other than a few sunburns from suddenly being outside with our families more often, something unexpected did happen after a few months. We found that (a) the quality of our work improved, (b) our timeliness for deliverables improved, and (c) our overall responsiveness to client needs improved, as well. All unexpected.

In trying to accurately assess these improvements, I spent a lot of time homing in on the enormous pressure we had long worked under and how it meant our schedules were usually maxed out. No time to spare. But in those times when an emergency or urgent client request would come in—which in the tech business was commonplace—we had no slack to handle it. Zero extra hours to throw at a suddenly urgent problem. So, we would try working double time and pulling rabbits from the hat, inevitably making errors of judgment in our exhausted states, leaving us on edge, tempers flaring. Far from ideal, and from it we learned that *organizational slack is important.*

It is the CEO who needs slack the most, and who is most often congested—all the more reason to be a role model for dynamic balancing. This sends the message out across the organization that slack time is valued because it is good for the company, good for friends and family, and good for everyone's health and well-being.

When slack becomes a scheduling dynamic, the CEO finds time opening up often for the first time, and with it, the mind is freed up to wander and wonder about business strategy and new opportunities—which is the first and foremost value a CEO can bring to the job, so a critical imperative.

Yes, the CEO should be, must be, the role model for dynamic balance.

Ethics, and Walking It versus Talking It

Though I've come to ethics last in this chapter, it is at the top of the intangibles that drive an LS to success and should most obviously be practiced with an almost religious fervor from the outset. Anything less invites mishaps.

I will fall back on that simplifier—description—rather than a definition of ethics, which could go on for pages and still be as thin as a worn dime. Descriptors are integrity, honesty, transparency, compliance, fairness, doing good, compassion, empathy, and truthfulness. With these descriptors, we find *talking* about ethics much easier. It's the *walking* of them that is especially hard. Especially when we look all around and see a broad cultural acceptance and even worship of lying, cheating, stealing, selfishness at the risk of others, bullying, and getting away with ill-gotten gains.

More precisely, when these kinds of untoward practices become commonplace and the competition is using them to get ahead on an unethical track, what to do?

The temptation is to say, well, others are doing it. What choice do I have if I am to stay in business? There is a logic to it, as far as it goes. In my own experience, I have found that by *not* succumbing to these base herd practices, by holding to the highest ethical standards, by working harder and sometimes much harder, even greater rewards come. That is where the logic can lead as well.

While I was still young, my older brother gave me an excellent perspective on the value of ethical behavior. He said that the punishment for the lying and cheating person is not being able to trust others. Being able to trust and being trustworthy are such joyful cornerstones of a fulfilling life that having those as part of one's life is worth the extra effort.

And so it was that many years after my brother's lesson, I was driving with my son seated next to me. In the distance, I saw a bunch of cars stopped on the side of the road, and wanting to avoid them, I sped up—a lot. At the other end, a police officer pulled me over. I tried to explain to the officer that the cars ahead of me were also speeding. My son then chimed in, "Dad you were *really* speeding!" The officer smiled and then wrote the ticket. Of course, my son was right. It did not matter that others were speeding. I was the one stopped.

But there is a deeper moral here involving my son's value system. Had I talked my way out of a ticket, that would have been the takeaway for him. Break the law and either don't get caught or wiggle out of any punishment. Not the lesson I wanted to leave my son with. Likewise, early in a startup, if the CEO is seen cutting corners for whatever the reason, the employees will be watching and internalizing these problematic practices.

Again, to reiterate my brother's lesson, one of the punishments for the lying and cheating person is not being able to trust others. Trust is a great simplifier. It enhances the effectiveness of decision-making and thus allows an LS to remain lean, saving a lot of time and resources along the way.

CHAPTER 4

TAKEAWAY PRINCIPLES AND VOCABULARY

- Create a lexicon that nurtures and evolves the company culture.
- Learn to deftly repeat without seemingly repeating.
- Be clear that the founder(s) also work for the company.
- Business objectives, not the owner's interests, are the starting point.
- Practice situational leadership.
- Aim for hierarchical decision-making but flatter communication networks.
- Flat networks improve information flow and decision-making.
- Practice interruptibility—be interruptible by colleagues and interrupt colleagues.
- The antidote to combinatorial complexity is judicious simplification.
- Develop a high tolerance for ambiguity and uncertainty.
- Make more effective decisions after socializing them with the team.
- Embed in the culture the preparation of decision agendas.
- Make assumptions, then validate in multiple ways.

- ⮑ Practice teach and learn, learn and teach.

- ⮑ Make the most of the team's talent with split-suiting.

- ⮑ Know the ways of diffusing power.

- ⮑ Have a board to check and balance the CEO.

- ⮑ The CEO should be at arm's length with accounting, finance, contracting, and legal.

- ⮑ Authoritarian and consultative managers are both needed, and having both augments situational leadership.

- ⮑ Organizational slack is productive and is attained through dynamic balancing.

- ⮑ The CEO must be the role model for dynamic balance.

5

GROWTH—WHY, WHEN, HOW

Aim to grow or aim to be? That is the existential question facing every business. And if the aim is growth or even hypergrowth, what are the objectives for the expansion? That is, why do it? To look at these questions, let's engage in a little complexification before simplification.

In the mid-twentieth century, business schools began expanding, the MBA degree gained a new *cachet along with it*, and new theories about organizational development were gaining purchase. Those decades lacked the powerful computing we now have, however. It seems quaint now, but great solutions were being worked out with pencil and paper. If only to ease writer's cramp, it became necessary to simplify, simplify, simplify.

These new all-encompassing business dictates sought to emulate the sciences, and so they were expressed as neat, simplified equations. Preferably one equation per business function, as scientists had done with their laws of nature.

From this a popular formalism emerged, called constrained optimization, and it became one of the cornerstones of a new field, operations research, a.k.a. management science. In a nutshell, this new science called for identifying the objective(s), identifying the constraints (time, money, capacity, people, space, etc.), and then finding the optimal solution.

So how to apply this new science to a company that serves many stakeholders?

There are those holding a financial interest—shareholders, creditors, landlords. There are employees, families of the employees, and retired employees as well. There are customers, neighbors, and institutions that factor in, be they nonprofits or trade groups. There are governments at all levels with agencies for taxation, for regulation, for assistance. This is, in short, a lot of people with a lot of different interests to consider in this so-called "constrained" attempt to optimize the enterprise.

So again, how to actually do it?

In the computation-poor, equation-crazy 1950s, it became dogma that the objective of the firm is *profit maximization*. And the companion objective for that was *maximizing shareholder value*. Both are mushy concepts, really. At best, they are qualitatively quantitative concepts that may strike you as an oxymoron, because they are.

I have always been amused by the quantitatively precise measurements of profit in a financial statement that is prepared laboriously. The so-called bottom line of a large company might be expressed in millions of dollars down to thirty-one cents. That's precise, all right. Yet in the laborious work, all kinds of assumptions are made that, if made just a wee bit differently, could alter that bottom-line figure not just by pennies but by millions.

Assumptions are made to depreciate assets—straight line or accelerated? To decide on historical costs—over which periods? To write down nonperforming assets—on which basis is default computed? To project a reserve level for future returns—using deterministic, stochastic, net premium? And what of 2002's Sarbanes-Oxley's mandatory mark-to-market of some assets and liabilities? The list of assumptions fills pages. So, at the end of the day, as they say, are those precisely measured profits just qualitatively quantitative or even truly qualitative?

I remember a case where an incoming executive who had little financial acumen was told by accounting that the bottom line could be tailored to what he wanted for the year. That surprised him, and when he asked how, he was told that he would not understand—it was all quite complex!

So, the executive asked me, and I went to talk to the folks in accounting. It turned out the company had big pension funds for the employees. The future obligations of those funds were subjected to present-value analysis. A dollar tomorrow is less than a dollar today because you can invest that dollar and get more than a dollar tomorrow. How much more depends on the interest rate. The reverse computation, that is how much you would have to invest today to get a dollar tomorrow depends on the discount rate. So, going forward from a dollar to its future value is based on the interest rate. Going from a dollar tomorrow to its present value is called the discount rate. Same modifier.

The discount rate that is used to calculate the present value of new future pension obligations determines the hit to the bottom line, a component of employee costs. To get to the bottom line of the executive's desire, accounting was going to use the discount rate to get at the deduction from the bottom line that would give the desired number. This is a common manipulation and only one among many available to accountants. To lend an air of respectability to these manipulations, accountants are keen to footnote their assumptions and normalize their calculations, but even a nonfinancial type can readily see the true fluffiness of profits that have been measured to the penny.

So-called shareholder value is even more ambiguous, and any effort to maximize it is even fluffier. Never mind being able to measure it; what does maximizing it mean? For the current reporting period, for the next reporting period, and all the reporting periods ahead, in which case, are we talking about present value, and if so, what is the discount rate? Is the same discount rate applied, or does it adjust for each period depending on the anticipated inflation rates?

The reason for running through this rigmarole is that these concepts lie squarely in the path you'll tread as your company emerges as an LC.

Understanding that metrics sold as "hard" are usually "soft" may give you a little more comfort when describing (always describing, not defining) the objectives you are aiming toward and the metrics that will drive your own progress.

The reality is that every firm is pursuing multiple objectives. So, the operative concept becomes constrained optimization on a multi-objective level, and this means making trade-offs. For instance, some companies describe themselves as employee oriented, others emphasize community friendliness, others are environmentally conscious, and others are impact driven. Each of these many objectives requires that trade-offs be made.

Once I was challenged by a buttoned-down CEO who insisted he was dedicated to profit maximization at all costs. "No ifs or ands or butts out of those seats—we maximize around here, dammit!" Colorful and compelling he was. So, I told him I wanted to run a scenario by him, to get his feedback. "The SVP walks in and tells the CEO he's sorry to report that he just returned from the doctor and has been diagnosed with dementia. Clearly, he's going to be an increasing threat to profits. Shouldn't the CEO immediately let him go and recruit a replacement?"

Mr. Button Down went silent. What I had not said, though we both knew it, was that this terrible diagnosis had recently been given to *him*. So, should he tell the board he was stepping down at once? In the silence that followed, I think we both gained a better recognition of the truth that even profit maximization can be a fluffy concept.

Character of the Company

Many of the principles we've looked at have shaped the character of the companies I've been affiliated with: I also work for the company … business objectives come first … teach and learn, learn and teach … customer success first, then satisfaction … since money is like a power outlet that only becomes useful when appliances are connected to it, make money but also make an impact … and by the company, through the company, and for the company.

My entire reason for leaving academia and going into business was to field test a sweeping premise I had that the right set of principles could support not one but many objectives and stakeholders and lead an LS to becoming a viable LC well poised for an impactful RE.

Did I succeed in testing out this whole sweeping premise?

My decades-long field validation has led me to believe so. As well, many of the people who worked with me at Kenan Systems have gone on to form their own companies guided by these same principles, offering another level of validation.

So then, will they work for you similarly?

There are many paths up the mountain, with some more likely than others to land you on top. I have tried to map out the "likely" paths based on decades of teaching and fieldwork. Hence this guidebook.

But you be the judge.

We've all seen companies put their principles up on the wall in framed posters, and there they apparently sit. I recommend that whatever principles you do adopt, put them on the wall if you wish but definitely put them into practice, monitor them, modify them as needed, and never forget them. That is how they become embedded in the company fabric.

And do it iteratively, with noisy exploration, bringing a tolerance for ambiguity and uncertainty to the effort, always keeping in mind that the traditional metrics of business success depend on so many assumptions that they may appear quantitative and precise but are largely qualitative and fungible. So, don't take them too literally.

L or L?

In this journey from LS to LC and beyond, we have been clear that the L stands for *Lean*, which makes the entity more efficient and makes an RE more likely but does not, of course, guarantee it.

A great number of CEOs will, as soon as resources become more abundant, want that L to stand for *luxurious*. Sweet digs, executive perks, a company jet, limos for the senior staff. Oh, and mahogany, lots of mahogany.

Such a path can also work. In addition to my own experiences, I have biases. I've lived the immigrant experience, having come from Turkey, and I know what it's like to build up from nothing. And I've lived in the Boston area for decades; the spartan character of that city's Puritan heritage has rubbed off on me.

Boston proper counts about six hundred thousand residents and the metropolitan area about three million, or just under 1 percent of the US overall. Yet its reach is unbounded and in a specific way.

About 20 percent of all the assets under management by US investment firms are handled by Boston-based companies such as Fidelity, State Street, and Wellington. *Lean* operators, for the most part.

Boston has top-rated cultural and educational institutions—the Museum of Fine Arts, the Boston Symphony, MIT, Harvard, Boston University, Tufts, Brandeis, Boston College, and many more. And they share a common thread—they are all private! It shows the level of wealth and philanthropy of this *lean* city.

And of course, Boston boasts four of the leading sports teams—the Red Sox, Celtics, Patriots, and Bruins. All *lean* performers, usually.

I've been affiliated with MIT for many decades—as a student first, of course, then on the faculty, and now as a board member. Anyone who visits the campus can attest to its *lean* culture—notwithstanding its architecture, which has journeyed through utilitarian minimalism and over-the-top exuberance. Despite the exteriors, you can venture down any of its many corridors and be amazed at how spartan the offices and labs look. The students and the faculty are dressed to fit: somewhat spartan and not fashionable at all.

As Boston and MIT have accommodated me for sixty-plus years, I have ample evidence for the power of *lean, lean, lean, lean*. Others may put the L to other uses such as *luxurious, lofty, laudable*, and of course, one need not be confined to one L. But for success as I've known it, my money is on *lean*.

Timing and Perception of Growth

In growing a company, it is important to keep a keen perspective on the nature of time, so as not to be tricked by it. For instance, an initial success can distort future successes. Our minds are wont to extrapolate an initial success into future progress exponentially. Reality can be more sobering.

I saw as much often in academia with students' doctoral theses. A student might make excellent progress in the first six months and then project that out another six months only to find himself still struggling after many years.

Similarly, an LS that has doubled in size (by staff count, orders, revenue, whatever the critical metric) every year for the first few years is likely to assume the trend will continue and will plan for such growth by hiring staff, leasing extra space, etc. In planning for this exponential growth, the team becomes even more convinced it will be so. And should anyone request proof, they can point to the pudding of the first five years' results.

But then comes the dreaded plateau. Sales stagnate, and profits vanish. All that newly leased extra space is sitting vacant, and all the added staff is underutilized. To highlight this potential false expectation of finishing soon and planning for it by leasing extra space and hiring staff, I made the following part of the vocabulary: *The first step is 80 percent of the way (really hard to get going), but so is the middle, and more importantly, so is the last step.*

Yes, it does add up to more than 100 percent, a lot more, and that is the point. So many times, having completed most of the project, the anticipation might be that the last step is going to happen quickly. Yet so many times, it is that last step to the finish line that keeps taking longer and longer. This convoluting of time can happen at each level in the business—from R&D, through development, through go-to-market.

Death in Green Valleys

It is often said that paths to success for startups go through the valley of death, reminiscent of the wagon trains headed west in early America. This is a very real ordeal that startups face, properly evoking sympathy and support. But there is also a lesser-known valley of death—the green valleys.

These green valleys are places of ostensible success, and all who arrive here should be proud of their accomplishments. They've made it. Only now do they get to meet the natives of the green valley who resent newcomers and can be fiendish in trying to contain them or, failing that, destroy them. Silicon Valley's streets are littered with the remains of these once shiny-faced newcomers.

Upon the success of becoming an LC, there are often throngs cheering the milestones achieved. But once that success is clear for all to see, different emotions surface. Associates begin jealously demanding a larger share of the sweet pie. Clients know they can be tougher in negotiations. And big companies that had once ignored your calls or laughed you off now take direct aim at you. And with the resources they have to muster against you, this becomes the biggest threat you've faced yet.

At this point, the success you're enjoying could be quite a fragile one. Let's dig into this question from another angle.

If the company's foundations are fairly weak and the culture that's holding the team together and aligned with the company strategies is not well formed, a "let it be" strategy may be the smartest strategy.

It may be best now to focus on consolidating all the successes that have been achieved and hardening against a competitive environment or unwelcoming economy.

It may be best to work for a level of resiliency across the organization, a holding pattern of sorts.

Such an approach should not be discounted since, at this point in time, you have 100 percent of something. But should you attempt to kick the engine into overdrive, you risk that 100 percent becoming 0 percent.

So, let's talk about keeping it lean in the green valley so that survival and later a giant leap to success remain doable objectives. With this in mind, the first principle must be *Don't expand resources ahead of growth.*

I came to this early in business when a seasoned executive gave me two bits of wisdom. One, never run out of cash, or else, he warned too knowingly, you're off to the penalty box and out of the game. And two, budgets once approved are certain, while revenue remains probabilistic. So, he advised, make expenses dependent on revenue.

There is much to be said about budgets being static while revenue is dynamic. The first and most obvious is that it results in periods of overcapacity followed by periods of undercapacity. This translates into another shoutout to AAWE because with this hiring approach you have staff that are more easily repurposed. They have the A (aptitude) and the W (willingness) to learn. Situational leadership coupled with the practice of staff repurposing makes the organization more flexible and dynamically adjustable to the variable workload. I call this a dynamically reconfigurable organization, and it's vital for keeping the LC lean.

Postsales Maintenance Impact on Growth

Your path to growth will continue to be driven, logically, by the nature of your offers. Some offers don't require much in the way of postsales maintenance. If, however, maintenance is required, then recognize that the cost of establishing a field network of service technicians could become burdensome and crimp growth if not well executed. This field service expense could offset any new revenues generated, since field service expenses run at a premium.

Alternatively, and still worse, if the offers fail once in the customer's hands and cannot be properly rectified by the field service crew, the company's reputation takes a hit along with future sales. This kind of in-the-field judgment on your company can happen so much faster with online ratings and rankings that are now pervasive and accessible by all.

Underselling versus Overselling in Sales

Given a choice of a sales team that's underselling versus overselling, the choice is always the latter. But caution is in order. Underselling leaves a lot of revenue on the table and leaves the company failing to hit its marks while threatening margins and profit targets. But overselling is equally problematic.

A seasoned executive once related to me how his company's overly aggressive sales staff had put the company on the path to ruin because the company couldn't support all the extra sales; they fell behind in deliverables, and service teams ran weeks behind schedule. It became a capacity nightmare.

Judging Effective Capacity

Say a rapidly growing LC has fifty on staff, and ten are added to deal with a 20 percent increase in sales. The capacity increase therefore matches the need, right? Well, even if the new additions have the requisite skill sets, they do not begin with company-specific knowledge and must be trained. Assume it takes a month and three full-time equivalents (FTEs) to handle the training. From a management perspective, the 20 percent capacity increase might seem sound except that for that first month, the net capacity is forty-seven, not sixty. And that one month becomes the period when problems in production, quality, and delivery are most likely to happen.

Growth in revenue must be managed in tandem with growth in capacity, in people, in facilities, in support services, in every facet of the operation.

I once taught a business case in which this dynamic was entirely lost on management. The company in this case manufactured kitchen appliances that they then wholesaled to distributors who then sat on that inventory for several months on average before then selling it to end users at retail. For years, there had been few, if any, quality issues. Then in one period, there appeared widespread reports of product failures.

Panicked, management added QA staff to that product line. Those staffers needed to be trained, which the existing QA staff would do. But then that lowered the number of bodies devoted to QA during that training period. So, with fewer bodies, the QA fell off and nobody knew if defective units were being shipped out to distributors to once again sit in storage for months.

Several months did pass, and all seemed fine. The extra QA workers looked redundant and costly to management, so they returned those added workers to their previous lines. Then *wham*, new reports of product failures ... because those last-shipped units were finally being purchased at retail, and clearly that temporary falloff in QA had mattered. Management had to lurch back into a repeat of the crisis-response cycle. A random, one-time event became a costly cyclical production nightmare.

This seemingly minor observation about a company's gross versus net production capacity can indeed have serious consequences—especially just when the LC is growing and can least afford bad customer ratings.

Organic Growth versus Acquisitions

When growth is imperative, making acquisitions can be tempting. But it is critical to first think through the long-term ramifications of acquiring another company for its talent, or its capacity, or even to gain market share.

Just as a customer can leave an LC with customs and if it is a customer with bad habits, the LC itself can get reverse infected ... the same can happen with acquisitions whose culture and practices can create clashes. If the acquired company is an aggressive, power-oriented, ethically flexible outfit, the acquisition could seriously hamper the LC—even if revenues suddenly grow. In time, the acquiring LC can end up falling hostage to a new culture—as if the LC itself had been acquired.

My recommendation is that especially in the early stages, an LC aims to grow organically. Once it reaches a reasonable size, then acquisitions can be safer—especially if those acquisitions are much smaller in size.

Naked Acquisitions

Acquisitions in an M&A context typically refer to the merging with or acquiring of a company with its staff, customers, assets and liabilities, and intangibles as well. However, there is also a concept I call a naked acquisition, and it can be a very interesting tool for growth.

Acquiring a patent portfolio, either by purchasing or licensing it, is an example of a naked acquisition. An LC can also acquire the distribution rights of a product already on the market, or rights to both manufacturing and distribution. These naked arrangements, which happen without the people in the company being included in the deal, can be a far more effective strategy than acquiring a company lock, stock, and barrel. And if people are needed, they can be hired on a contract basis.

I, myself, accidentally ended up with an acquisition like this, and after a few stressful months, came to appreciate the naked nature of it.

At Kenan Systems, we had been using an advanced software platform called Stratagem; it was the commercial version of XSIM developed at MIT (sensing a thread here?). We had licensed Stratagem for our internal use and for developing and delivering several systems to clients based on it. We were all in. So, we were rocked to the core one day to learn that Stratagem had just been acquired by Computer Associates, leaving us stuck up the proverbial creek for all we could tell.

We leaped into crisis mode and in our research, discovered that years before, Stratagem had bifurcated its source code and sold one branch of it to the Mars Corporation. Yes, the candy company, which is still privately held with revenues of $40+ billion. After first using the platform internally, Mars had then wrapped a company around it named Acumen, which developed first-rate decision support systems for several companies in the UK.

Even before I could reach out to Acumen, coincidentally they contacted me to let me know that they were keen on expanding into the US, had heard that we used the Stratagem platform and that our success in building massive systems was based on that, and so would we be interested in entering into what they called a "deep relationship"?

I took that to mean we would be able to use the platform to continue our projects and solve our problem, so yes, I was ecstatic.

They invited me to meet with them in Maidenhead, UK, their headquarters. When the president and his associates joined me at the table, so too, did a senior VP of Mars who was headquartered in McLean, Virginia, who "happened to be in town." Okay, I thought.

Within minutes, it was clear that their idea of a deep relationship was for Kenan Systems to fully acquire Acumen and all its thirty-five staff members, most of whom were located in Maidenhead.

"It's a hard pass," I told them, trying not to sound perturbed, despite being clearly blindsided. We simply didn't have the cash for or interest in that kind of transaction.

The Mars senior VP encouraged me to produce an offer anyway, so I came in with a lowball. Jaws dropped, unsurprisingly. Nonetheless, the VP said he'd take it up with the two Mars brothers, Frank and John, who together with their sister owned the company and actively ran it. Apparently, Acumen had served its purpose and they just wanted to give it a good new home.

A few weeks passed, and the senior VP called to say they had checked out Kenan Systems and concluded that we were the right home for Acumen, which was more important to them than money, and they would accept my offer, with four caveats. The deal had to close in two months. We had to open an office in the UK. We had to take over all the clients. And we had to make offers to all thirty-five staffers.

That should have given me pause. But naïvely, I opted to proceed. We did open an office in the UK and transferred two of our formerly Cambridge-based staff there to prepare for thirty-five new employees. I right away set up quarters in a quaint inn there in Maidenhead and started interviewing the Acumen staff next to a toasty fireplace.

I gave about forty-five minutes to each, given the time constraints. And each was more competent than the last—a talented bunch, yet somehow discontented, sullen even, which was disconcerting. Still, I pushed through, interviewing them all and then formally extending offers of employment to them all as well. We didn't just hire them outright because the Mars Company had told them that if they didn't want to join Kenan Systems, they could stay on with Mars for up to a year.

Not one of the thirty-five staff accepted our offers.

I was flabbergasted and set out to see why. I soon learned that in the UK, job interviews are done very differently. A job position comes with a well-defined job description. The selected candidate goes through a variety of tests and meets with supervisors and goes through multiple interviews. All this might take a day or even more. Against this backdrop, my forty-five-minute fireside chats struck them as insincere, even disingenuous. They thought they'd be hired only to be let go shortly after. In the end, we hired only one person and then only on a contract basis.

The result was by default a naked acquisition, which became a huge advantage. Had it gone the other way, clashes between the Acumen and Kenan Systems cultures could easily have been damaging along with the payroll burden and administrative hurdles of fully operating in a foreign country.

Plus, the price I'd offered, which had been inordinately low, was now just right for the platform we acquired. What we also acquired was a well-seasoned product in the marketplace. With Stratagem, we had the software to use but not the source code. With Acumen, we had both.

Interestingly, the Mars company had also made a naked acquisition in that they had acquired a duplicate of the Stratagem source code, named it Acumen, and built the staff in Acumen, the company.

Naked acquisitions can be a powerful way to grow an LC and keep the culture intact rather than potentially fractured with the sudden infusion of staff (even if, or especially if, you don't back into it the way I did).

Growing in Place versus Branching

Whether or not you should branch out your offices and capabilities is another important question to address, one driven by factors including your offers, your markets, your customer types, and their geographic distribution.

I advise growing in place until there is great confidence that the company culture, communication networks, and business and technology structures are fully stable. While still in one location, you can run trial-and-error scenarios in a relatively safe setting. I call this organizational stratification. Let me explain.

At the LS stage, there is usually less concern about who is doing what. There's a lot of roles overlap mixed with teamwork mixed with situational leadership mixed with jack-of-all-trades activity going on pretty much around the clock. But as the staff grows, the specializations follow in accounting, legal, HR, and so on, and with that comes organizational stratification. At the macro level, there are the technical staff, the production staff, and the support staff. Then, for example, drilling down into the technical staff, there are engineers, then there are senior engineers, principal engineers, computer engineers, etc. Each staff cluster has similar strata. So far, so good.

But as the strata build up, the assignment of appropriate titles for individuals can get tricky. Once titles like senior or principal or staff accountant, principal accountant, or staff lawyer and general counselor get locked in, there's no walking back. Unchecked, this *title inflation + organizational stratification = communication obstacles + power problems.*

With so much stratification trying to creep into the organization, it's far better to manage it from a single location. If the independent variable of distance and its siloing effect is excluded from the mix, it is easier to work through the kinks. Everyone is in the same room, and it is more easily handled.

At least two dynamics are usually at work in these titling exercises. One is an employee's justification for a title. For instance, a customer-facing salesperson might want to be called a senior executive so she can impress the prospects, or a unit manager might want to be a vice president to enable better dealings with outside vendors. And soon you have a lot of chiefs in title only. In terms of the underlying jobs, there might not be much difference. But to the employees themselves, there is.

Another reason for this stratification is the attempt to attract better hires by offering them fancy titles. If entry-level people are given great-sounding titles, naturally the titles of the existing crew will need to be stepped up too. Before long, everyone is a VP or in the C-suite.

Stratification creep—be really careful with it. Because it can create a top-heavy organization in titling and with that, a subtle expectation among employees that their core job responsibilities are now beneath them.

When I was at Bell Labs, I was impressed by how deftly they sidestepped these issues there. They called everyone "member of the Bell Labs staff," and there could be no higher honorific, as if rolling chief strategist, lead analyst, wizard-in-residence, and le maître all into one title, but no bowing allowed. Navy SEALs is another example. Being a SEAL says it all.

Hand in hand with title stratification comes location and space stratification, deciding who sits where and how much space they get. Naturally, those with higher titles want bigger offices and in choice locations. Soon, the company is multilevel, with the C-suite up on the higher floors with the bigger offices.

In extreme cases, I call this "dollar-bill management." On the back of the dollar bill there is, as we know, a pyramid with a seeing eye in the apex.

Euphemistically, I liken it to top management ideally seeing far and guiding the organization in the pyramid below. The problem is, the apex of that pyramid, which is supposed to be guiding, is *not connected* to the rest of the pyramid! Whoops!

Well, of course, the dollar bill's designers did that purposely. They meant for it to represent an unfinished structure, symbolizing the US as a young nation continually striving toward perfection, ever with room for growth and improvement. Great symbolism for a country, and for a business as well to never stop trying to bring the strata closer together, better connected, and more functional! But as symbolism goes, that seeing-eye apex is disconnected on the dollar bill and just as often in the executive suites of US companies.

I recall visiting a company that was located in a handsome circular building. In the lower levels of the building, there were the lower-strata employees. In the top level, there were the five members of the executive team, the seeing eye of our dollar bill. The office configuration was pie shaped with a central core where elevators opened to the five offices of executive secretaries behind glass windows floor to ceiling. Each of those secretaries' offices had a mahogany door in the rear leading into their respective executive's suite. Each of those five executive offices then opened out to a shared exterior balcony. So, each executive effectively had a corner office as well as a shared meeting place separated from the minions. It was the ultimate in dollar-bill management, a bitter vision of how capitalism can revert to feudalism, and so yes, leaving a bitter taste in my mouth.

The polar opposite of this configuration is cubicles for all, with the only offices being conference rooms and meeting rooms that can also be used by the staff requiring privacy for phone calls. This configuration is my preferred choice, as I noted earlier. And these choices do matter.

The stratification in titles, location, and staff can have a profound impact on whether the LS becomes an LC, and remains one. There is no imperative to remain lean, but my advocacy is such. And not just because I'm a proud Boston bean. Also because of the keen advantages it affords in terms of resilience and agility—which are critical in the fast swim of commerce.

At the most basic level, the argument *against* overstratification is the argument *for* the principle that everybody works for the company. It creates a more inclusive culture: a sense that we are in this together, we have each other's backs, nobody is above the law. This becomes a cultural badge of honor that everyone wears. And with everyone acting in unison, it creates a more resilient force of nature. That's the ideal ... even if not perfectly executed. It is certainly worth striving for. And in the striving, another big benefit naturally bubbles up to make a difference: agility. Agile creatures are noted for their arms and legs acting in unison, efficiently. That's what this ideal is all about too.

When it comes time to branch out, growth through branch offices and capabilities can be a good option as long as focus is kept on the objective of the branching—is it for extending, functionality, duplication, or layering?

Extension Branches

Extension offices are just that, extensions of a company's central location. One could even view a separate floor as such. When the COVID epidemic forced massive experiments in office locations and layouts, some of these remote learnings and habits continued. In a real way, homes have become extension offices and the main office merely a convening center.

This is, for now anyway, reversing a trend of past decades of having hundreds, if not thousands, gathered in a single location. Many a high-rise tower has been built for just that. Economies of scale, proximity, and ease of communication are the justifications. Post-COVID, and with video conferencing, we have entered the era of extension offices.

This is a net plus for staying lean. Companies can now operate on a hub-and-spoke basis that's enjoyed by all. It allows a healthy melding of professional and personal interests for the entire team. But the downsides are very real, beginning without the "out of sight, out of mind" issue. There are other issues that we'll get into as well.

Functional Branches

An example of a functional branch is a service center, production center, or customer support center where proximity of functionality creates efficiencies. Setting up functional branches is straightforward; managing them is not, as we'll see.

Duplicative Branches

Sometimes growth is supercharged by duplicating the main office in another city, state, or country. These are clone offices, usually smaller in size. As such, they can be given a lot of autonomy and even act as independent entities.

Layered Branches

Any of these branch types can act as mini-hubs or mini-branches that offer advantages such as a localized presence or more responsiveness. This is a structure that embodies the maxim "think globally, but act locally."

Each of these branching types can and likely will grow to become quasi-independent divisions of the company. The mechanics of operating these divisions are fairly straightforward with a cursory knowledge.

Risks and Legal Structures

Branches do introduce unique risks that can be contained by organizing them as nested LLCs. This requires only minimal legal and tax maneuvering, and the basics are straightforward. Having these nested or layered structures will make a later exit, rich or otherwise, much more manageable.

As always, simplicity should be the guidepost in creating these branches. I'd much rather focus on the performance of the company and pay the fair share of taxes that come with it than expend countless hours on fancy schemes that make financial planners your partners and complexity and organizational bloat their handmaidens—the antithesis of lean.

Pillars for Successful Branches

- In placing the pillars of a successful branch, we again turn to the principles of a successful main office:
- AAWE for hiring
- disempowered but highly supportive HR, legal, and accounting
- leads belong to the company and are accumulated in marketing to be assessed for fit with company strategies and capacities
- separation of marketing and sales with a triage mechanism to allocate the filtered leads in marketing to the sales staff
- revenue is by the company, through the company, for the company, which is especially important for the farthest-flung branches to understand
- company culture articulated in a lexicon
- excellent documentation of the offers
- situational leadership
- everybody works for the company, including those who have financial ownership
- in decision-making, start with the business objectives

I view this collective of principles as the fundamental pillar of starting lean and expanding lean. If all these principles are well established at the home office, then their conveyance to the branches becomes easy.

A second pillar is the maintenance of these principles, which relates, in a way, to the differences between humans and computers.

When a row of numbers needs to be added up, a computer will do it exactly the same way over and over. Not so a human being. We humans tend to veer into noisy explorations of alternatives. Even in something as straightforward as addition, we'll often evolve our procedures and assert our individuality. It's our human nature.

Left alone, the company's branches will tend to do the same. They'll evolve on their own, develop their own culture and their own lexicon, and look less and less like the LC back at home base. This is not necessarily unhealthy *unless* it has the effect of dividing the LC into an array of mini-companies. So, maintaining the company's principles through strong feedback loops is important.

And even more than in the central office, you must be wary of the power dynamic shifting. It is tempting for a branch manager to develop her own power base. Power is alluring, addictive, and sticky. In due time, the branch manager might view the staff as *her* staff rather than a team she is also a part of, and most dangerously view the leads and the revenue as *hers*.

Prototyping for Branching

When a branch office is warranted for, say, getting closer to a major client, entering a distant market, or tapping into the labor pool of a less expensive labor market, simple prototyping can be useful.

As the branches evolve, this prototype can also evolve into a model of future branch offices. Many tools can be adapted for such a prototyping-to-models approach. The CEO's participation in these efforts is absolutely essential at each stage—from interacting with the branch leaders going into the launch, to early-stage setup and monitoring of systems and operations, to regularly checking in and ensuring that the company's culture is ascendent in these new locations.

Aiming for Consistency across Branches

There is an inherent rub in an LC branching out. That comes from trying to maintain a level of consistency in the branch organization's performance while still encouraging localized situational leadership and initiative. To manage for this balance effectively, we return to the core-and-shell concept.

This is a rather universal concept, as we discussed in the transitioning of custom systems to platforms. Nature uses this model extensively. Our own immune system's cells can adapt to pathogens with the cell's core remaining the same but the shell adapting to or learning from the pathogens.

In companies, the core can evolve as well but at a slower pace. Be that as it may, the CEO has a job to do at this stage that's essential to keeping that desired level of consistency across the branching company. It's a job that a CEO may understandably think is no longer necessary since the LC's culture and mores are fairly well rooted at the mother ship. But culture doesn't travel unaided.

It becomes necessary for the CEO to spend time moving around a new branch office, engaging with individuals and groups, and describing (never defining, always describing) the LC's core culture, architecture, and practices. Then, the CEO must return regularly to ensure that the mechanisms are functioning to maintain the desired consistency.

I used to do that by hopping from branch to branch and holding staff meetings packed with preambles on culture and illustrative stories, the cornier the better in my case because that was my own storytelling style and it better engaged the teams, made all the information sharing more enjoyable, the lessons stickier.

Opening a Training Academy

While my branch hopping had some effect, there was always a super-ficial quality to it. A CEO can only hop around so much, and at one point, formal training programs need to be established. In due time at Kenan Systems, we formed a training academy through our Denver office and put new hires through an intensive program in our culture, lexicon, business practices, etc.

Key people in our branches would also spend time in Denver periodically as part of their continuing education. We viewed this as no less important than professionals like lawyers and accountants being required to accumulate continuing education credits. To keep our professional standards high and our culture ascendent, we not only ran drills on the basics but also studied new developments in our markets to be better prepared.

We sought a college-level sophistication in our training programs, believing it essential to our continuing success as an LC bending toward an RE.

Growth through Partnerships

In addition to growing through branches, an LC can grow through informal partnerships formed for specific purposes such as jointly bidding on a major project, linking arms with others in channel part-nerships, or even forging deeper ties in joint ventures.

Personally, I've found partnering to be a complex and taxing enterprise in the main. With few exceptions, these partnerships can trigger a clash of cultures and business practices. I urge caution, and yet there can be good reasons to enter into them.

Partnering as a Team Member

Teaming with another company to bid on a project, for instance, for a big RFP (request for proposal) is quite common. When the LC is ready, this kind of arrangement can be quite productive. However, there should always be a solid teaming agreement in place.

Earlier I noted the importance of understanding key components of contracts and being involved in the writing of them. Same for teaming agreements. The noteworthy components are as follows:

- The roles—prime versus subcontractor
- Flow through of T&Cs to the prime and the subcontractor as well
- The division of work among the parties
- The rates that will be charged
- Audit rights and processes
- Conflict resolution—courts or arbitration and the jurisdictions (New York or Amsterdam or Singapore or ...)
- Breach, and its remedy
- Termination and assignability
- If the RFP is won, the clauses of the teaming agreement to carry forward
- If the RFP is not won, whether the teaming agreement will expire or be modified for subsequent RFPs

A well-constructed teaming agreement can make the partnership solid and create a great deal of synergy in combining resources. A poor one can lead to years of anger, conflict, and bitter accusations. Like long-fuse bombs, the agreements can appear fine until much later when a single overlooked clause now becomes explosive. By investing a few hours up front to develop a first-rate teaming agreement, you can preempt downstream issues that could trigger many hours of unproductive unpleasantness. An ounce of prevention …

Here is a practical suggestion. Take a pro forma teaming agreement from an online source or your lawyer. Spend a few hours highlighting the clauses that seem important. Even if you are not directly involved in the negotiations, when the draft agreement is before you, you'll then be able to quickly assess it.

Entering into Joint Ventures

A more permanent teaming is a joint venture. The same issues apply, only amplified because the stakes are higher. Decisions to be made include these:

- Who plays what role?
- How is revenue allocated?
- What happens to the initial and subsequently developed IP?
- How will assignment, breach, liabilities, taxes, termination for cause, termination for convenience, and all the standard contract items be handled?

This time, the two companies are joined at the hip; thoroughness matters.

Value of Channel Partnerships

In any industry, there are a great many distributors, consolidators, retail outlets, and system integrators that can be effective channel partners to accelerate growth with minimal additional expense, though at a sacrifice of unit margin. However, if greater volumes can be obtained than the LC can obtain alone, then there's a big bump to the bottom line from channel partnerships.

Again, you are well advised to be knowledgeable about channel agreements. For instance, if an *exclusivity clause* is built into the contract but market demand suddenly grows and the channel can't handle that, what had been a growth generator now becomes a growth obstacle.

Also, a *markup clause* might at first appear innocuous, but if competition begins slashing prices, the only way to compete might be to cut margins on offers sold through channel partners. In the examples of both these clauses, building in some flexibility in the beginning can pay off down the road.

Growth through Company Acquisitions

The most radical path to growth is by acquiring companies, something that requires a lot of caution, patience, and tolerance for ambiguity, and even then, most such unions end up as failures.

Most acquisitions fail *not* because the business fundamentals are unsound. The failure may come because people up and down each organization didn't buy into the deal. Just because the apex bought in doesn't mean the pyramid did. It's more like a zipper that gets closed at the top while the rest of it won't close or won't stay closed. Not good. And all these issues are only amplified by the Herculean task of smoothly integrating the customers, vendors, suppliers, and other stakeholders.

Since M&A is difficult and risky, any thought of entering into an acquisition should come only after partnerships have been thoroughly maximized, naked acquisitions have also been maximized, and the LC is confident it can remain lean or is prepared to leave lean behind—for almost surely that will happen when the acquisition is completed. If a, b, and c are in order, then an acquisition done properly offers the potential for hypergrowth and can advance the LC toward an RE.

CHAPTER 5

TAKEAWAY PRINCIPLES AND VOCABULARY

⊃ Know if or when the *L* should still stand for lean.

⊃ Capacity-increased growth lags can be ruinous.

⊃ When capacity is being increased, existing capacity declines during the training period.

⊃ Is organic growth or acquisitions better suited to the organization?

⊃ Naked acquisitions grow the company less disruptively.

⊃ Beware the death lurking in green valleys.

⊃ The first step is 80 percent, but alas so is the middle step, and so is the last step.

⊃ If you run out of cash, you are taken out of the game.

⊃ Make budgets dependent only partly on revenue.

⊃ Don't expand resources ahead of growth.

⊃ Work toward a dynamically reconfigurable organization.

⊃ Title inflation + organizational stratification = communication obstacles + power problems.

⊃ Underselling leaves revenue on the table; overselling is a path to ruin.

⊃ Know how to best branch out to new offices and locations.

⊃ Understand how to handle partnerships, joint ventures, and channel partners.

6

DIVERSIFICATION

Grow or not? Diversify or not? Two intertwined questions and we just briefly offer some additional perspective on them.

Internal Diversification

Perhaps the easiest of all paths is internal diversification. If there are new market opportunities that could be addressed by adapting some of the offers in the portfolio, an LC can present the relevant offers inexpensively modified to these markets and take it from there. A term for this is re-contexting with adaptation.

Market Diversification

We've talked about how platforms and core-and-shells can be used to architect offer portfolios. Platforms and core-and-shells can also be re-contexted and adapted to enter new markets inexpensively and speedily. If the LC has maintained a robust internal offer development engine, it can create offers/products specifically for these markets.

Adjacency

While a new set of offers can be developed to diversify into a new market, this may also require that a new organizational structure be built to support this initiative. A less burdensome solution may be to use adjacency.

Adjacency is derived through inputs, outputs, or both. A classic example of input adjacency comes from P&G. Legend has it that candlemaker William Procter and soap maker James Gamble married the sisters Olivia and Elizabeth Norris. Their father had noted that both his sons-in-law used the same input—fat—and suggested that they become partners. Hence, P&G.

P&G morphed input adjacency eventually into output adjacency. At its peak, the number of brands primarily in beauty, healthcare, home care, and family care markets had reached a staggering and sprawling 150-plus. All from a vat of fat. Then in 2015, CEO Alan Lafley elected to sell off one brand after another, leaving P&G with just sixty-five brands for what he accurately called "a much simpler, much less complex company of leading brands that's easier to manage and operate."[12] Adjacency returned, now through simplification.

Divisionalization

When input and output adjacencies can be intertwined, advantages present themselves. For example, one division can sell to another division through transfer pricing. These divisions can still both exist as profit centers. To do this, sales incentives can be built in to ensure that both teams take full advantage of the adjacencies. Yet the setting of internal transfer pricing can get sticky. Here's an all-too-common example:

---

12   Rachel Abrams, "Procter & Gamble to Streamline Offerings, Dropping Up to 100 Brands," *New York Times*, August 1, 2014, https://www.nytimes.com/2014/08/02/business/procter-gamble-to-drop-up-to-100-brands.html.

If the supply division's transfer price has high built-in margins, it then makes a lot of money, and that means fat bonuses for that team. They like it. But it comes at the expense of the selling division, whose prices need to be competitive out in the marketplace. So, the selling division management complains loudly, fairly accusing the supply division of jacking up internal price tags on items, lacking efficiency, or just being lazy, pointing to the external suppliers (which they could be using!) that offer the same product at lower prices.

How, they complain, is the selling division supposed to be competitive in the *real* marketplace when the company's competitors have access to cheaper supplies? The solution, in their view? Let us buy from our inside supply division and from outside sources as well, choosing whichever source offers us a better deal.

So what should management do in this situation?

An initial step might be to provide a subsidy to placate the selling division, but that can quickly grow into an administrative nightmare, while not fully satisfying anyone. Another step is to allow the selling division to procure externally, in effect becoming like a buying company within the company.

Now it is the supply division's turn to complain. They could go ahead and admit that they are a monopsony of sorts, a sole supplier, and quite capable of applying pressure on their internal customer, the selling division. But frankly, they're angry that the selling division has been squeezing them by threatening to turn to external suppliers unless prices are dropped in their favor. There's bad blood, and the supply division begins threatening to retaliate by supplying others outside the company—even if that isn't management's desire.

So, what is management to do in this situation? In fairness, the supply division's request to sell externally should be granted.

But now the selling division is again up in arms, because the company they all work for is being hurt by the supply division selling externally, taking away sales that the selling division could, because it is their core expertise, do much more efficiently.

So, what now is management's play? Well, they could go back to square one and merge the two divisions under a single manager. Reintegration.

I've seen this dynamic play out and completely distract otherwise competent teams. The problem is, there is often no good solution. So, it may just be best to leave the divisions be and let them sort matters out.

At this point in our journey together we've tracked your LS becoming a full-fledged LC with multiple offers in multiple markets and an expanding network of branches and divisions. All great. But if this expanding entity cannot be adequately maintained, it's all for naught. So, we'll look at that in part III.

CHAPTER 6

TAKEAWAY PRINCIPLES AND VOCABULARY

- ⊃ Diversify by re-contexting and adapting offers to new markets.
- ⊃ Platforms and core/shells can be re-contexted and adapted to new markets.
- ⊃ Use adjacency for more successful market diversification.

ON THE PATH
TO EXIT (OR NOT)

1

PURSUING EXCELLENT, OR AVERAGE?

Being excellent. That has been my measure of success and my aspiration for going on nine decades now. And yet, apropos, a time back I was gifted a keen insight from one of my graduate students at MIT. After the lecture, this young man cornered me and pointed out, rather confrontationally, that the target audience for my course syllabus seemed to be those who, according to one measure or another, were deemed excellent and then in the top quartile of that. And yet, he noted, the median IQ of the population was one hundred, and, relevantly, many of those with average IQs went on to accomplish great things in their lives.

Was there a credibility gap in my work?

It was good food for thought. And as I strolled back to my office taking the long way, I considered the young man's implied criticism that my teachings were just too dang elitist to be of any real value.

It was certainly true that only a few students graduate with a straight-A grasp of the material, yet many more go on to grace the covers of industry magazines. Also true that I'd never seen a definitive correlation between high grades and high performance in the workplace. And there were plenty of stories of people who never finished college yet went on to become superstars in their fields.

What if excellence is a noble metric, yet not an ideal one to pursue?

That thought rocked me in my young professor's shoes. And the more I thought about it, the more I evolved in my thinking in favor of a concept known as multiobjective optimization. We touched on this earlier, but I came to believe that in a business sense, a company ought to pursue excellence in most instances, averageness in some, and humdrum occasionally.

On the personal level, there is a relevant time-worn adage: Know who you are and be who you are, progressing to who you want to be—because nobody can do that better than you. This is a cheat sheet for multiobjective optimization. It means that in college, you may have been an average student, a superb athlete, off the charts as a poet, and a capable explorer. Now on this individual level, it may feel like the professor is prattling on about the obvious. And I am ...

Yet, in easily grokking this personal application of multiobjective optimization, it then becomes easier to understand its less straightforward business application. Specifically, how many LCs today continue to measure their performance by relics of the equation-rich, computation-poor midtwentieth century: profit maximization or shareholder value maximization, which can be limiting measures.

Multiobjective Optimization

As an LC grows, a CEO tries to remain attuned to the interplay between objectives and constraints, and to lead accordingly. This is the stuff of strategic management. And one doesn't need to hire McKinsey or Bain to advise on this. A combination of noisy exploration, judicious simplification, and ambiguity tolerance can go a long way.

This thinking about optimizing, given the company's objectives and constraints, may sound like a quantitative undertaking. But it is quite qualitative in nature. And by employing the right vocabulary, you can lead the company toward the right combination of excellence + averageness + humdrum.

Let me propose a vocabulary and accompanying spider chart for it.

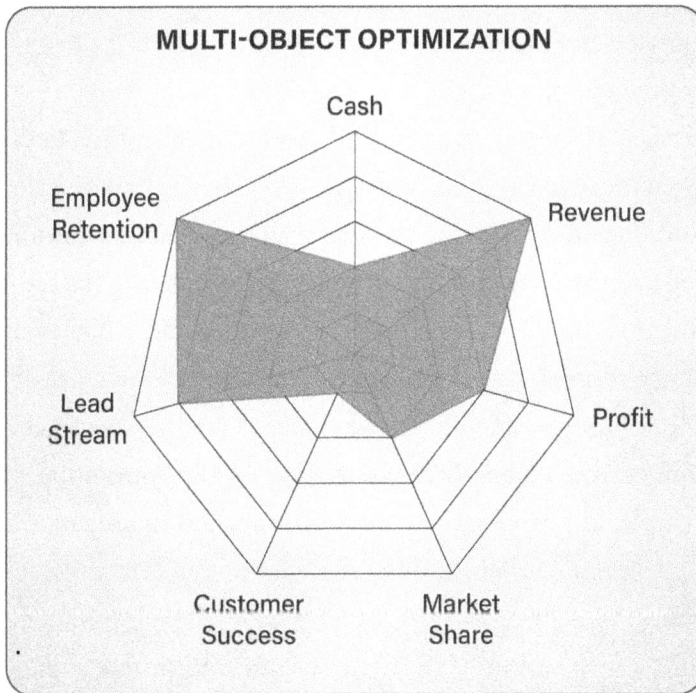

Figure 7.1. A spider chart can function as a framework for mapping out the correct path to a Rich Exit.

As you see here, the chart's radial lines emanating outward each represent a critical value such as cash, revenue, profit, market share, customer success, lead stream, and employee retention. No priority is given here—we're assuming for this example that all are important. Likely these seven values are the important ones for an LC, though you may prefer a few different values that better measure performance in your specific industry. Or you could have two of these charts to gain precision—one for quantifiable values and the other for more qualitative values.

In the discussion to come, I'll use the term *excellent* to refer to the complex of objectives even though at the single-objective level, *optimization* might mean aiming for average on the spider chart of values. (Like the student who aims for a B average but on the basketball court pushes the envelope.)

So, the questions begin.

What if you aspire to average profits but excellent market share?

Or average customer acquisition but excellent employee retention?

And on and on through the spider chart we could continue.

Your approach to these intertwined questions will, in fact, drive the kind of Rich Exit you later enjoy. For this becomes a framework for mapping out the strategies that enable the kind of Rich Exit you seek.

The values you choose on the spider chart may not necessarily skew financial. A company can be average on the bottom-line values, for example, but excellent in an expertise such as unique machining or tool development/fabrication. That choice may well drive the exit you seek.

In my own ventures, I viewed revenue and profits as values to be advanced respectably but not maximally. Other measures, such as innovating the kinds of seminal systems that could potentially have a big impact, and validating my professorial pontifications in the real world, were more important to me as head of Kenan Systems. So, they drove the kind of Rich Exit I enjoyed.

In figuring all of this out, there's little need for complex equations and formulations while at the LS stage or even for an early LC. A spider chart of the company's values becomes a qualitative framework to serve the purpose. However, as the size of the LC increases, *values* must yield to *metrics*.

Metrics for becoming excellent and remaining so.

There are many ways to assess the health of an LC—not only for management's needs but for outside parties' interests as well.

Financials. Standard financial statements include a balance sheet, income statement, and cash flow statement. All essential.

Nonfinancial metrics. You can truly shape the character and the personality of the company by choosing what these nonfinancial metrics should be.

Visualization. Visualization tools and techniques have become very important. I use spider charts for summary views and then drill down with an assortment of charts. Also, the power of generative AI can be tapped to create new views on the company's data yielding new insights and opportunities.

Outside validation. External check-and-balance tools can be valuable outside validators, helping to steer the company clear of unanticipated troubles. When a young company is still operating as a single-member LLC with no bank debt, then an outside audit can be optional. However, I still recommend doing it.

Formal audits by reputable accounting firms are expensive affairs. Much less expensive and almost as useful is a simple review. With both an audit and a review, the financial data comes from the company, and in both cases, the management needs to certify the accuracy of what has been provided. The difference between the two is the audit letter. That's what increases the price substantially. So, with leanness in mind, settle for doing a review until later when a Rich Exit looms on the horizon and audits will then be mandatory.

Another outside validation is an ISO certification. This is an independent group that evaluates the organization along several dimensions. It is similar to the spider chart in the findings that will be presented. If the company is doing any manufacturing, ISO compliance lends a number of advantages.

Many professional organizations also provide audit or review services for a fee. These could be even more useful and informative than ISO audits.

Then there are benchmarking firms that compare the company to industry norms and competitors. This can be highly useful in charting the growth course of the LC and in reassessing the spider chart of objectives.

Hybrid Validation

MIT's year-after-year excellence and top rankings are a marvel. I have served on its board for almost a quarter century and observed and participated in one of its little-known but highly effective validation processes, visiting committees.

Each department in each of MIT's five schools prepares a comprehensive self-assessment to be submitted to the visiting committee. The committee is chaired by a board member, with members nominated by the board, departments, alumni, and students. The review lasts a day and a half. Findings and recommendations are then orally presented to MIT's top management—the chairman, president, provost, and dean. Lastly, the committee chair makes a presentation to the full board.

In preparing for the visiting committee review, the department drills down to fully assess its progress against objectives, processes and procedures, issues, weaknesses, assumptions, and their asks.

It is highly effective. I recommend a variation of it not just for the LC but also for the LC's divisions and branches. The visiting committee could comprise experts in the industry, outside consulting firms, and amenable professors.

The resulting findings and recommendations can inform the company's strategic plan going forward, and the very act of a CEO having to answer to such a high-level external review puts every strategic initiative in the company under the glass to beg for its justification. Even if the external review nets only a handful of recommendations that sway the thinking of the CEO, the exercise will have proven useful.

Adapting and Evolving to Remain Excellent

Once excellence has been mapped to the company's objectives and then achieved, and the party hats all swept up, the task of maintaining a high level of excellence gets no easier. Even excellence can become static once attained, and we know a static organization can ossify and quickly fall out of step with the world around it. Evolving and adapting are essential for remaining excellent.

So how best to translate this insight into action plans going forward?

An Ideal Kind of Innovation Culture

Often, innovation is confused with invention when, of course, they are very different things. Our focus here is on innovation for in a dynamic world, an innovative mindset is essential to sustaining the LC.

There is a less-considered confusion about innovation, and it is this: innovation can be a big, jarring thing but it doesn't have to be, and shouldn't necessarily be. Indeed, when innovation leads to a big, jarring step-change, it invariably triggers counterreactions. I've found that innovation that instead leads to baby steps forward can be more effective. I call this incrementalistic innovation. Whatever one is working on, then, explore ways to make it just a little better.

With incrementalism, every part of an LC can be improved with the whole organization truly even though the perception is that there's been no change. Change but no change becomes the approach to take; it can even become a generalized strategy.

Having this incrementally innovating culture doesn't mean everyone is free to innovate and implement their innovations on a whim, of course. Certainly, the assembly line is no place for running a new idea to ground. The practice of innovation is always going to be context dependent with the company's commitment to building opportunities for innovation in all the right places made clear to all.

A critical stage for successful innovation is the feedback loop that must be in place. Without feedback, there is no way to evaluate results and decide whether to adopt the innovation, give it another go-round, or just abandon it.

Feedback as Part of the Culture

The feedback loop is important in the context of innovation, but of course, it's just as important for feedback to be embedded in the company's every activity.

There are many feedback loops, both internal and external.

External feedback is now widespread. The internet, with its social and commerce platforms, has embedded feedback of one sort or another into nearly every communication or purchase decision. This feedback is so omnipresent that it is almost impossible to order something or receive a service such as a car repair without getting an instant survey for feedback (with an implicit or even explicit request to rate the provider a 10 out of 10).

Internally, the team's performance reviews can become an excellent two-way feedback mechanism. Earlier, I advocated for the

CEO to get deeply involved in performance reviews and mentioned using something I call GRRITS: goals, responsibilities, requests, interests, talents, and skills.

This GRRITS framework goes beyond the usual performance reviews, treating the process as a two-way street. In the process the CEO not only assesses the employee's performance to date, but the employee also assesses the company's performance. It works along a four-item agenda:

GRRITS PERFORMANCE REVIEW OUTLINE

1. Looking back on the team member's performance

   - Team member provides a self-assessment.

   - Reviewer comments on the self-assessment.

   - Reviewer provides an assessment of the team member.

2. Looking back on the company's performance

   - Team member assesses the company's performance.

   - Reviewer comments on this assessment and provides edifying feedback as needed.

   - Reviewer comments on team member's perspectives on the company.

3. Looking forward on the team member's performance

   - Team member articulates what he/she aspires to and wants to be doing in the coming period.

   - Reviewer takes notes on the requests of the team member for later consideration.

4. Looking forward on the company's performance

- Team member makes requests of, and suggestions for, the company.

- Reviewer outlines company plans/strategies/issues for coming year.

Upon completing this assessment—gaining a clear view into the employee's own goals, talents and interests, and requests of the company—the assessment can then become a morale boosting and teaching and learning opportunity for the rest of the company.

All the positives that came out in the employee's review can be shared with the entire organization at the next all-hands meeting, and the negatives from the review can be left solely with the employee to quietly work on bettering.

This process can also be an excellent way to identify innovations individual employees have driven, assess the potential of those innovations for the organization, and then spread them across the organization when it makes sense.

This entire process does take work. But it is far from an onerous exercise with minimal rewards—just the opposite, in fact. At Kenan Systems, we learned to handle it quite quickly in the course of things, and in so doing, we created a much deeper network of shared trust in the company.

All in all, it was good for building up an employee's self-esteem and good for the organization. Highly recommended.

Praise Reappraised

We should also lay bare an often-negative aspect of employee performance reviews, so this aspect can be considered and hopefully dispatched early on. I'm referring to praise. These days, and especially with millennials, "praise sessions" are all the rage, meant to amplify the best in people. But do they really?

In a seminal article in the *Harvard Business Review* in 1963, Richard Farson pondered the question of why some people actually got *defensive* when praised.[13] Shouldn't they be *delighted* instead? Farson came to some interesting conclusions:

"Praise is not only of limited and questionable value as a motivator but may, in fact, be experienced as threatening. Rather than functioning as a bridge between people, praise may actually serve to establish distance between them.

"Instead of reassuring a person as to his worth, praise may be an unconscious means of establishing the superiority of the praiser. Praise may constrict creativity rather than free it. Rather than opening the way to further contact, praise may be a means of terminating it."

Two key explanatory theses of Farson's are that praise will be seen by some people as the sugarcoating for negative comments to come ("We think the world of you, and that is why we are relocating you to the North Pole"). Farson's takeaway from his research was fundamental: it is better to build and maintain trust and let the praise take care of itself.

In my experiences across decades, I have found many of Farson's timeless assertions continually applicable. I have found that extending trust and, in turn, being trustworthy carries far more water than constructive praise. Just about every expression of genuine trust becomes a great simplifier, preempting so much of the ill will, conspiracy theories, and corrosive behavior that cannot hold a candle to trust, wisely extended—that is, verifiable. Here is an example illustrating how trust or the lack thereof can affect interactions:

---

13   Richard Farson, "Praise Reappraised," *Harvard Business Review*, September 1963, https://hbr.org/1963/09/praise-reappraised.

A manager who is rarely communicative is in an especially good mood one day. As he walks down the hall, he greets an oncoming direct report warmly and says, "Isn't it nice that it's so sunny today" and moves on.

However, he notes that the report looks at him blankly. If there is trust, that is the end of the matter. If there is mistrust, the report goes to his office wondering what the heck is going on since his boss is not usually so effusive. Is a sinister plan afoot? He starts texting his pals in the office, asking, "Is anything amiss?" The boss, for his part, is back in his office puzzling over that blank stare. He starts calling around, asking "Is all well with my team?" Soon this very innocent encounter in the hallway between boss and subordinate triggers waves of speculation. Those who were texted or called begin calling and texting others, and out it snowballs!

An important point here; actually, two. Certainly, being consistent in your ways can be more important than you might casually think. And second and more to the theme of trust, whenever there is an opportunity to give feedback, do it in a mutually trusting environment such as teach and learn, learn and teach.

On Beliefs and Counterevidence

As humans, we are fond of hypothesizing. (This is what happened! This is what might have happened! This is what could happen!) We can spend hours doing this with friends, family, and mentors, getting their views, telling them ours, watching the news, or dipping into the dark web to run down our hypotheses. One might expect that as we collect more and more data and discover that our hypotheses miss the mark, we abandon them and move on. That's a logical thing to think.

Only humans aren't logical.

If we get a hypothesis firmly embedded in the old noggin, and especially if we sourced this hypothesis from an authority we trust, then it becomes a belief. It can even become a core belief and a cornerstone of our worldview. And once a cornerstone is in place, only an earthquake can rattle it.

We all have these hypotheses running around our brains, and we all, to a greater or lesser extent, have come to take them as beliefs, established truths, verities. And they impact how we respond to a new situation.

Let's say we are presented with counterevidence to a hypothesis we've long held. If we find the data valid, we may abandon the hypothesis quite easily, depending on the context. For instance, if we've long thought that the town we live in has 3,500 households but then Census data comes out and the number is 4,124, we can accept that without pushback.

This is an easy context. But many are not.

Take the contemporary example of climate change. No matter how much evidence of climate change, both anthropogenic and otherwise, that some people are presented with, they think it's all a bunch of hooey. And why?

Neuroscientists have identified the chemical processes at work in our brains that cause this stick-in-the-muddishness. When our core beliefs are challenged, those beliefs can intensify and any challenge to them becomes suspect.

There is no magic resolution to this human foible, but it is super important to keep it in mind when giving and receiving feedback. Because if people's predispositions are not accounted for in these feedback mechanisms we've been talking about, then the mechanisms will not yield anything useful.

Conflicts, Protests, and Resolutions

As the LC grows, adapts to market realities, and branches out to seize new opportunities, as surely as the seasons change, all kinds of "authority nets," as I call them, will start getting tossed all around. Type X and type Y managers will have a go at each other. The smallest departmental crises will suddenly become the CEO's immediate problem. And so having a handful of conflict resolution strategies at the ready will be helpful.

If the LC has grown significantly, these problems will be simply too big for the CEO alone to resolve. At this point, some formalized conflict resolution mechanisms should be set up not only in HR, their natural home, but distributed across the organization.

Returning to the notion that no core belief can be toppled by counterevidence, if an interoffice conflict is somehow rooted in a belief set, then there's no sense trying to reason your way through to a resolution. Not going to happen. In fact, it may make things worse by layering on a new distrust of management.

Sometimes conflicts flare into protests. Labor union–backed protests that lead to strikes are a well-known example. But companies have many less-obvious protests going on all the time. Some are rooted in internal conflicts, and others are just stubborn-headed belief systems playing out. If not properly handled, these somewhat silent protests can get out of hand and cripple an LC.

More complex are the sympathy protests. When a social demonstration becomes a media event, however far away or removed from the company's day-to-day, employees may want to launch a protest in sympathy.

What to do? A protest can peter out all by itself, persist without doing much harm, or really get out of hand. Back to the walking-with-coffee example. Any kind of intervention must be in sync with the protest dynamics.

The actual response, however well synced, must always be coming from a position of trust. Having established a culture of trust and transparency from the outset, you are in the strongest position to resolve conflicts that come up.

Several times I have brought up the value of situational leadership, and this becomes another instance. A side benefit of having this leadership practice embedded in the company culture is that a disgruntled employee can be moved into a transient leadership position in certain situations to resolve an ongoing conflict. Some conflicts arise because an unhappy staffer is upset over a local matter and can see no resolution—but only because she lacks the broader context. So, step in, toss an imaginary set of keys to her, and say, "You don't like my driving? Okay, instead of being a back seat driver, you've got the keys now, and you drive this organization for a stretch."

Amazing what a shift in perspective can do to a person.

Here's a repeat of an example I gave earlier, now in the context of a protest. Say the plan is to go from point A to point B, which, on some imaginary graph paper, is in the upper-right quadrant at a sixty-degree angle. The shortest path is a straight line from A to B at sixty degrees. To an employee with only a local perspective, that line may appear crooked, so he wants to make his segment of the line run horizontally for a bit, even though it blocks the whole plan to get from A to B efficiently. Worse yet, if he is unable to fix the crookedness that is so obvious to him, he may come to see management as incompetent, even crooked. That becomes his core truth, his belief. And from there, it's one small step to finding colleagues who concur and two steps to a protest.

I faced this situation many times. On one occasion, an employee made it an ethical issue on the grounds that if he went along with what he was asked to do, he would be violating his professional ethics. Instead of providing counterevidence, I just shelved the project. However, if the issue were one where I could have made the employee a situational leader, he may well have seen the broader context in a new light.

Growth, Complexity, and Innovation

As growth happens, complexity increases toward combinatorial complexity. (Yes, it just keeps coming up!) If the team is being overwhelmed by all the complexities they face, the usual solution is to hire more staff, retain more consultants and contractors, or add more square footage to the office. These solutions may well alleviate the burden; they may just as well add unneeded bloat. I advise judicious simplification before deciding on any kind of capacity increase.

Innovation is desirable. Being innovative is the mantra. However, being innovative is the original double-edged sword. Along with all its potential benefits come a host of unknowns, uncertainties, and complexities of every stripe.

Take a car, for example. If the carmaker wants to add a cool new engine part because it offers benefits over the old part, then all the surrounding parts can be affected. The design, installation, and maintenance documents have to be modified. Extensive field testing will surely be necessary. New supply sources might need to be found with supply contracts negotiated. The assembly workers may need retraining. All the benefits that a single new part might bring might be more than offset by the additional complexities as well as the additional cost of the surrounding impacts. This is one big factor why innovations die on the vine.

By the way, when the pride-and-joy innovation of an engineer is deep-sixed, and the engineer doesn't know why or in what context the decision was made, that engineer can be expected to conclude two things: management does not appreciate him; management is dim witted. A big seed of discontentment has been planted, one that could grow into a big organizational protest. So, handling the people behind the innovations is as important as the innovations themselves.

One way of steering toward the light is to always be trying to innovate toward simplification. Innovating for improvement is good and fine. But innovating for simplification can yield handsome rewards. Let's look at why.

Judicious Pruning with Employees

Going from LS to LC to RE seldom happens along a straight, cleared, or forecast pathway. Many times, it is one day at a time despite the best-laid plans. To reiterate, planning is essential, but plans must be dynamically adapting.

Adaptations by their nature render so much obsolete. Ethernet cables were once built into the walls with outlets at each desk. Then wireless routers replaced them entirely. Examples like this can go on and on, but the hardest question is how to handle these adaptations when they render employees redundant?

Certainly, repurposing can help. If the LC is applying AAWE, incremental innovations, teach and learn, situational leadership, and GRRIT reviews, repurposing becomes so much easier, natural, and powerful. But what if, even after extensive repurposing, there are still members of the team no longer able to effectively contribute—generally through no fault of their own?

Staff reductions are, of course, always painful. Often, management will try to sidestep the pain—especially if specific individuals must be terminated—by instituting across-the-board reductions. This is likely to upset even more people than solve the problem and may well trigger new problems. It is invariably best to have established internal trust and transparency so that when hard business decisions must be made, the team is more likely to understand. In which case, selective staff reductions will be more effective.

CHAPTER 7

TAKEAWAY PRINCIPLES AND VOCABULARY

- ⊃ Engage in multiobjective optimization.
- ⊃ Conduct internal, external, and hybrid validations.
- ⊃ Make incrementalistic innovation a part of everyday operations.
- ⊃ Conduct performance reviews using GRRITS: goals, responsibilities, requests, interests, talents, and skills.
- ⊃ Install distributed conflict resolution processes and mechanisms.
- ⊃ Aim to innovate toward simplification.
- ⊃ Run training to turn resilience into a mindset.

8

THE JOY OF EXITS

Since there is such great joy in saying it aloud and in many hearing it …

At this point in your journey, you have taken your LC through trials and tribulations, navigated through the valley of death and into the green valley, battled the residents of that valley, and weathered attacks both external and internal. You may look upon your LC with tremendous pride because you made it when so many who started this marathon have fallen to the wayside.

Now you face what may be the biggest challenge of all: To exit or not, and if to exit, how?

Not an easy set of decisions.

First, there is the intent to exit. Then, there is the timing. Foremost, there is the how. So, intent, timing, and how. There are other lesser questions, to be sure. Sometimes, it is not a decision of your choosing but instead a reaction to an attractive unsolicited offer or a mandate from shareholders or funders with controlling interests. However, you have come to the exit, and if it is time to think it through, I can again wholeheartedly recommend doing some noisy exploration.

If the company has outgrown you or you can no longer maintain balance, perhaps you should change roles. For instance, if you are the CEO, maybe stepping into the CTO role and hiring a CEO or promoting someone from within to that role might be a form of exit.

If an exit is in the cards, you might not be the one to prepare the company for a successful exit. Situational leadership! Why not have someone take over for that final stretch?

If you created subsidiaries or acquired companies and kept them localized, selling one or more might be a good way to learn about the vagaries of a full exit. At Kenan Systems, I didn't do that, but buying the Acumen business from the Mars Corporation gave me a huge window into the M&A process. And when the big exit came, I was quite familiar with the ins and outs of M&A.

Another way of getting a preview of what's ahead is to simulate an exit by hiring a company that does M&A and going through the steps as though there is a buyer for your company. It is not so much about the specific valuation and negotiations but more about the processes involved. If this is done early on, you can get yourself better prepared to pull the trigger when the right time or the right buyer, or both, are at hand.

The IPO Option

IPOs are headline-grabbing events. As it says in the name, these are very public events! Lots of extravagance because it's undeniably true that while millions of companies are formed, only a handful make it to an initial public offering.

Since 1995, yearly IPOs have averaged around two hundred with a low of sixty-two in 2008 and a high of 1,035 in 2021.[14] So,

---

14   "Number of IPOs in the US 1999–2022," Statista, February 3, 2023, https://www.statista.com/statistics/270290/number-of-ipos-in-the-us-since-1999/.

across nearly thirty years, only about six thousand companies have gone public.

What is more surprising is that in 1996 there were about 8,100 listed companies; now there are about five thousand. That is a nearly 40 percent decline when one would have expected the opposite. Adjusted for population, it is more dismal. At its height in 1996, there were thirty listed companies per million people. Since 2010, it has been flat at around thirteen listed companies per million.[15] That is a 60 percent decline, and the numbers keep getting worse.

When you look at IPOs three years after going public, you find that more than 50 percent are underwater—trading below the stock price on IPO day.[16]

Also worrisome is that the median age of an IPO company at launch has gone up. In 1980, the median age was six years; in 2021, it was eleven years and appears to be increasing.[17] This translates into substantially more cost in reaching the launch gate.

Despite these odds, the IPO route is available and for the right LC, it may well be the way to go.

Getting Acquired (M&A)

With so many giant companies bent on growing through acquisition, a viable exit route is to merge with one of them. The transaction could be for the revenue and profits, in which case it is typically based on a multiple of EBITDA (earnings before interest, taxes, depreciation, and

---

15   Based on data compiled from the World Federation of Exchanges and the Census Bureau.

16   Kerry Sun, "Half of All 2021 IPOs Underwater after Record Year for Listings," Market Index, December 31, 2021, https://www.marketindex.com.au/news/half-of-all-2021-ipos-underwater-after-record-year-for-listings.

17   "As Companies Stay Private Longer, Advisors Need Access to Private Markets," NASDAQ, August 11, 2022, https://www.nasdaq.com/articles/as-companies-stay-private-longer-advisors-need-access-to-private-markets.

amortization). That multiple can run from three for a manufacturing company up to twenty for a tech firm in a hot sector. With a strategic buyer, the multiple can go higher. That's because the sale becomes similar to that company we visited earlier, where a developer wanted to build a skyscraper and needed to purchase the next-door parking lot to do it.

There are a lot of M&A companies that facilitate such sales. They tend to specialize in either EBITDA size or industry type, and sometimes both. The total value of deals during recent years has been around $2 trillion, but this is skewed by some very large deals. The number of deals averages around five thousand per year. It's good to keep an eye on the M&A deals pages to be aware of the trends. This is also a good way to keep an eye on the competition.

Private Equity

Private equity has become huge. They do have a model: buy a company, cut costs, increase cash flow, load it with debt (which shifts the risk to the lenders) and in about five years, sell it way above the acquisition price. To be sure, there are a lot of variations on this model, but the key driver is to strengthen an acquisition through debt capital for a sale in a defined horizon.

Sometimes private equity takes a partial interest, which of course is a complex exit that could keep you at your old desk much longer than you wish.

Search Funds

There is an evolving type of private equity called search funds that aim to buy companies that are heirless—the founder is cashing out, and the children have no interest in running the company on an ongoing basis. These search funds act as pseudo-heirs. Their targets are small-to medium-sized businesses. As baby boomers retire in vast numbers or want to, the companies they built become a target market.

If you want to grow through acquisitions and have the cash, you might either act as a search fund and go after heirless companies in your space or even search for search funds whose portfolios might have such firms.

Family Offices

As wealth has concentrated in the upper echelons, the number of family offices has increased sharply across the past decades. These offices offer the client family not just investment but tax planning, charity planning, succession planning, and even psychological services as well as mediation services to deal with intrafamily disputes and conflicts. Of interest to you is their increasing role as private equity providers. Currently, the family offices have more than $2 trillion under management in the US alone, and some of them are doing what private equity does: acquiring companies and portfolios of companies.

The Family Offices Association has a hundred-plus single-family offices in the US and is an excellent resource for gaining insights into potential exit routes. Their regular gatherings are attended by other CEO successes looking at next steps.

If the LC has reached a valuation of at least $50 million and $5 million EBITDA, joining a multifamily family office might help put your personal financial life in order as well as enjoy their many other relevant services. Then, whichever exit path you choose, your records are in order.

Foundations

If the LC is now prosperous with a significant cash balance and your interests have shifted to social impact and philanthropy, you can create a nonprofit organization and transfer some or a bulk of the LC to that entity. At your option, you can manage both. There are many forms and variations of this, and so if your interest is an RE via foundations or nonprofits or gifting the stock to an entity like a university, then perhaps retaining a family office that accepts multiple entities might be the way.

The Basics of Exiting

As we've talked about regarding HR, legal, and accounting, knowing the basics about exiting your company sets you up to manage the process.

Very likely, you will have an investment banker and should choose either a boutique firm or a big established Wall Street firm based on a number of factors, but most importantly, you should choose the one that makes you comfortable, for the fit will matter when the M&A machinery starts grinding and turning.

You'll want to have a general understanding of fee structures, deliverables, time frames, and exclusivity. Doing your research will put you in a good position to negotiate, and you'll be doing a lot of that.

Then there is the valuation. Again, many approaches. The most common is the forward EBITDA multiple or revenue multiple. The multiples used would depend on the comparables and the prevailing interest rates. As a side note, the inverse of the EBITDA multiple, which is a proxy for net funds, is the yield. So, if the forward multiple is 10, the buyer is expecting a 10 percent return. And if the forward EBITDA is expected to grow then the multiple could be higher.

In a straight acquisition, the LC is purchased outright. If the price paid is above the market value of the net assets, the excess is a premium for the going concern value of the LC and is booked as goodwill by the acquirer. It is then amortized over time. Until a few years ago, the amortization schedule was fixed. Now there is more flexibility. Either way, the annual amortization is a charge against the bottom line of the acquirer.

Since the acquisition valuation is based on future cash equivalents, what happens to the cash? And the value of the work in process? These often are matters of negotiation. Just knowing that could help you keep the cash.

More important is, what happens to you?

If you are deemed important to the business, the acquirer might want you to stay with so-called golden handcuffs and payments tied to milestones attained down the road. It's cleanest if there are no cuffs and you stay voluntarily.

Another critical matter is warranties and representations. There could be explicit and implicit liabilities, employee or customer or government lawsuits, warranties on products sold, etc. Who is to be responsible for all of these? The buyer wants you to retain some liability. You want to be done. So, it is a matter of negotiation. I suggest you go for what is known as *limited representations*. These limit the duration and amount of exposure you face, both of which have been assessed in due diligence, are well known to the buyer, and communicated in the purchase agreement you sign.

Some buyers want to burden you with the uncertainties, spread the payments over time, and tie them to the actual EBIDTA of the future years, which is known as an earnout. Better to resist such plans … unless you have supreme confidence in the buyer.

Another scheme, particularly favored by private equity, is to price the whole LC but pay for only 75 percent, leaving the 25 percent share in your hands along with a long list of restrictions, which make it worth far less than the full value.

So, get familiar with these constructs and then knowledgeably enter the negotiations that will determine the market value for all you've created.

Whatever choices you make at this stage, you have made even better ones to get here—you have attained a Rich Exit. Congratulations!

I hope some of the principles espoused in my first book and then illustrated in this companion guide have helped.

9

POST RICH EXIT— SO WHAT, NOW WHAT?

Depending on the nature of your exit, you could now face a variety of dilemmas. If the Rich Exit is widely publicized and the amounts are significant, you will be in the spotlight. You might enjoy that; you might not.

For me, being suddenly thrust into the public eye was less than comfortable. In the Kenan Systems merger into Lucent, I would have preferred it remained under the radar. Because Lucent was a public company, the matter could have been handled more quietly— which was my preference. However, because the transaction was accretive to Lucent stock, whereas a larger transaction Lucent had just made was dilutive by the same amount, Lucent announced the two proximally.

The point, of course, is that it's important to decide how you want to be positioned after the RE and build your intentions con-tractually into the negotiations so that some other outcome is not visited on you. If there is a press release to be issued, for example, have a say in it.

If golden cuffs are slapped on you, it's important to pay attention to the terms and conditions. Even golden cuffs are cuffs. In my case, I had no cuffs but volunteered to stay on as president of Kenan Systems as a wholly owned subsidiary and retain all the decision and management authority for one year. A year might be just about the right time. If you have a choice, best to leave after that and nurture a successor in that year.

Being part of a bigger company can be stimulating, but also hellish. A lot depends on how you manage the first few weeks or months. I would suggest viewing the acquirer as a customer and quickly drawing the cross and circle right away and setting about establishing links with the key people you've identified.

If you intend to stay involved with the business after an RE, keep it firmly in mind that your financial exit is not a business exit. You are still in charge, but your authority will be restricted. Especially if you have earnouts as part of the transaction, you are still in sales mode, so keep those noisy explorations for new sales revenues coming.

In acquisitions, the key people shake hands and forge solid relationships, but usually less so for the team down the ladder that has been swept up into a new company. They are now about to face often different accounting systems and practices, different HR systems and practices, different legal approaches, different office assignment practices, and all the intangible factors that collectively make a corporate culture.

Nobody is better suited than you to work on blending these two cultures as melodically as possible. This will mean adopting some of the buyer's systems, methods, and practices right away, planning for a reasonable period to adapt to other new company systems, knowing when the acquiring company can benefit from your company's cultural strengths, and gently pushing for their adoption.

My experience is that people can be transitioned to new ways much easier than systems can. Systems are like skeletons. Even nature has been unable to radically change mammalian skeletons from one species to the other, and it has a long history of trying.

When All Is Said and Done

Whether after a temporary stay in the acquiring company or a full-on exit, what then?

A lot of resources are now at your disposal, yes, and a lot of free time as well. The joys of an RE can quickly dissipate if the postexit period is not well managed. You can only dig your toes into the pink sands of the Bahamas for so long before wondering, "What now?" And so yes, the time to think about it and prepare for it is before the exit—but in a loose planning way, not in a fixed-plans way.

With an RE, suddenly your communities change both socially and businesswise. As does your family life. There is a saying that a woman marries for better or worse but never for lunch. Oh, how that has aged! The modern version is that each spouse or significant other has a life that only partly involves the other. After an RE you may find yourself home for lunch and inserting yourself into a life you've known little about, part of a family you've been absent from for too many years, and it can be wonderful … but only if handled properly.

With more wealth comes more responsibilities, and many new asks. A lot of people will suddenly want a piece of you. If not well managed, these asks could consume as much of your time as the LC did. If the financial asks are becoming complex, joining a multimember family office might make sense.

Or perhaps you still have a spring in your step and now wish to validate your legacy and undertake an all-new LS! You could set up a fund and go into the investment business. So many options!

Let me conclude by introducing a vocabulary word to replace the term *retirement*. I'm suggesting the term blending. Imagine your activities as forming a pie chart. At one time the LC occupied a big part. Now you have the luxury of turning the dial and rearranging what you will pursue next in your life.

I wish you a successful transformation of your RE to a fulfilling, gratifying new blend that will have made the journey from LS to RE truly worthwhile.

APPENDIX

THIRTY YEARS OF INTELLIGENCE EXTENSION (IE)

You may recall that I speak of artificial intelligence (AI) as intelligence extension (IE) since that's a more accurate descriptor up until such time that we all run into the so-called singularity, and best that we prepare for such an inevitability by holding the primacy of real intelligence over artificial.

And with that parting editorial, I can say that it has been a personal and professional delight to have been involved from its early days with what we now generally call AI.

First, as a student at MIT studying with Professor Marvin Minsky, whose theories on human cognition and machine intelligence made him a towering figure of AI.

Then, as a visiting professor in MIT's computer science department collaborating with Professors Peter Szolovits and Michael Dertousos, the latter of whom brought Dr. Tim Berners-Lee to MIT and spearheaded Web 2.0.

Then, at Kenan Systems, where we combined expert systems with natural language processing and big data systems to create among the first commercially valuable AI systems applications.

And now as a collaborator with my son, Kent Sahin, who elected to take the contents of my first book, case studies on Kenan Systems, and numerous other materials and turn it all into a handy ChatGPT utility.

Such a splendid cap to a long career—but of course, not a cap but another step along a path of innovation that has always, and will always, I believe, run through each of us.

Kent worked at Kenan Systems before starting his own company, REAL Software Systems, and turning it into an international leader in IP rights management. And now with Kent's ChatGPT – the Kenan Systems Way, you can ask any question and receive quick and rather accurate answers (increasingly so with usage, of course).

For instance, you can try prompts like "How can I apply the Kenan Systems Way to a situation in which my product demo crashes right at the outset of a meeting?" This is a common occurrence, of course, and an inside joke for our Kenan Systems alumni since it happened at one of our recent events!

ChatGPT – The Kenan Systems Way
Kenan E. Sahin, PhD, in collaboration with Kent E. Sahin
To access: http://bit.ly/KenanGPT

ABOUT THE AUTHOR

Dr. Kenan E. Sahin is an academic, scientist, inventor, technologist, serial entrepreneur, and philanthropist. Educated at MIT (BS, PhD), he went on to teach there, at the University of Massachusetts in Amherst (tenured), and at Harvard University. At MIT, Dr. Sahin received the Salgo-Noren Teaching Excellence Award. His focus has been technology innovation, development, and impactful industrial implementation. He holds fundamental patents on communication networks and advanced materials.

He founded Kenan Systems with $1,000 and grew it without outside capital into an international company with over a thousand employees, selling it to Lucent/Bell Labs for $1.5 billion. He then ran one of Lucent's commercial groups and became vice president of Technology at Bell Labs. The AI based telecommunications system he pioneered at Kenan Systems which Lucent renamed as Kenan/BP now processes a third of the global subscribers.

In 2002, Dr. Sahin founded TIAX again without outside capital to acquire the lab-based Technology and Innovation unit of Arthur D. Little when it was restructured after 116 years of operations. In 2014, he spun out TIAX's Advanced Materials division as CAMX Power. He serves as CEO and CTO of TIAX and CAMX. Both companies play key roles in their domains with CAMX having invented, patented, and licensed to key companies fundamental materials for lithium-ion batteries for use in EVs.

Dr. Sahin's awards include the World Economic Forum Technology Pioneer, the International Institute of Boston Golden Door Award, the Ellis Island Medal of Honor, the American Academy of Achievement Golden Plate, the Ernst & Young New England Entrepreneur of the Year, and the Richard Bolte Award for contributions to the chemical and molecular science community.

MIT's Dean of Humanities and Social Sciences and other professorships and fellowships have been endowed in his name.

Dr. Sahin's board service includes MIT (as a Life Member), Argonne National Laboratories, the MIT Energy Initiative, NEMA, the Boston Symphony, the Boston Museum of Fine Arts, AFS, and Robert College of Istanbul. He lives in Lincoln, works in Lexington, Massachusetts, and vacations in Kennebunkport, Maine, and Bodrum, Turkey.

ACKNOWLEDGMENTS

I am grateful to MIT for educating me as a whole person, expanding my mind in science, including industrial sciences, math, technology, arts, and humanities, and making me an integral part of its ecosystem. I meant to stay only for a short time, but after sixty-three years, I'm still embedded in the MIT environment. My time with and at MIT represents 40 percent of MIT's entire lifespan, commencing with an 1861 charter to be a "society of arts, a museum of arts and a school of industrial science," thus with a portfolio of offers that evolved through noisy exploration—two of the critical principles espoused in the pages of this guidebook.

In the richly networked ecosystem of MIT, I was honored to work alongside and learn from many highly impactful people, including its presidents, starting with Killian, then Stratton, Johnson, Wiesner, Gray, Vest, Hockfield, and Reif, along with its chairmen of the boards, including Johnson, d'Arbeloff, Mead, Reed, and Millard. Howard Johnson, Jerome Wiesner, and Chuck Vest served on my company boards and thus were mentors, colleagues, and friends.

It was the MIT Sloan Fellows I taught (and who taught me) for fifteen years who ultimately led me to start Kenan Systems as a field experiment to see if what I was teaching, pontificating, or just making up was really valid or just bullsh*t, as one Sloan Fellow once proclaimed. A few in the class agreed with him, the rest with me or had no opinion. That dramatic moment in due time would grow to a lot of self-doubt and hence the urge for field validation via a start-up.

After that one-person company began growing, I contacted many of the Sloan Fellows, and they continued to guide me and, when warranted, challenged me by pointing me and Kenan Systems to tasks that many before had failed to tackle. We ended up "drinking from the fire hose", a phrase used to describe the MIT experience, during and after, and popularized by Dr. Wiesner.

As such, the MIT Sloan Fellows were substantially the inspirators, mentors, and enablers of Kenan Systems as well as thousands who joined that company across its long lifespan.

Back in 1886, another MIT student, Arthur D. Little, launched his namesake startup. It took him nearly twenty-five years to turn the corner and become what many claim was the first technology consulting and transfer company in the United States. In 1935, per Little's will, Arthur D. Little, Inc. (ADL) was gifted to MIT, where it was transformed into a greater technology powerhouse. In the early 1950s, ADL was spun out. Once again a private company, it expanded its size and impact.

After 116 years of operations, this heritage company came to an end in 2002; its assets were divided into five parts and auctioned off, one part being the extensive laboratories and other assets of the "classical" ADL, which had become the Technology and Innovation (T&I) unit embedded in this three thousand-person company with branches in thirty countries.

I bought the assets of T&I quite by accident and then folded the staff of three hundred that previously worked for it into a startup I had founded, TIAX (Technology and Innovation Accelerated with X, hence TIAX). Overnight, TIAX, the startup, morphed into a restart of a heritage company.

With the validation in an environment so intertwined with MIT, I invited Dr. Charles Vest, MIT's president at the time, to chair the

TIAX Advisory Board. He honored me by joining in 2002 and served until leaving MIT to become the president of the National Academy of Engineering in 2007.

Since no outsiders wanted to invest during TIAX's first decade, I decided to make it another field laboratory to continue validation experiments now in a restart setting. Thus, what was in 1982 meant to be a short-lived validation initiative in the "real" world, has now been going on for thirty-two years with me as the sole shareholder and thus able (and willing) to run many trials without the usual concerns of fiduciary responsibility to outside investors' money or, more importantly, without their interference—a rare luxury and privilege.

The restart validation continues on and shall be chronicled in a subsequent book. But many of the learnings are already reflected in these two books.

In addition to MIT, MIT Sloan Fellows, and Kenanites (a name they chose), I am deeply grateful to my family, particularly my sons, who became unsuspecting participants in this validation quest. A special gratitude to Kent, who gifted me a Zoom call on my eightieth birthday—which included my former colleagues and members of Bell Labs staff—twenty-two years after leaving Kenan Systems when it had then become a wholly owned subsidiary of Lucent/Bell Labs.

That Zoom call transported me back in time and inspired me deeply. It was then that I learned that the key product of Kenan Systems—Arbor/BP, renamed by Lucent as Kenan/BP—now services more than a billion telco subscribers, or about a third of the global market. Clearly, the torch had been carried forward.

Kent and I followed parallel paths after we left Lucent; Kent started his company and also was the sole shareholder applying, experimenting with, enhancing, extending, and richly adding to the principles of KSC. His "experiment" also succeeded with that company being an international powerhouse in its space. Shortly after my first book came out, Kent created a ChatGPT version using that book as well as numerous articles and cases on Kenan Systems. That appears in the appendix. So very appropriately, the authorship of this guidebook is "Kenan E. Sahin, PhD, with Kent E. Sahin."

I am also grateful to Forbes Books. They put me on the path, with Lee Troxler designated to assist me with writing. I would write the drafts (for each book)—alas, in a dry, academic, lecturing manner. Lee would make the drafts more easily readable and, as appropriate, add content. Indeed, Lee acted as a co-editor alongside Katie Smith for the first book and Elizabeth Kennedy for this one. The guidebook benefited greatly from Elizabeth's perspectives on organizing the book into a more logical and practical framework, as well as from her pointed comments that strengthened the foundations. Designer Matthew Morse created the cover with really minimal input from me, and Heath Ellison as production editor coordinated the front matter, the copy edit, layout, and more to make it more cohesive.

I know there are many errors of omission and commission and so many omissions because of space limitations. That said, when I left Lucent in December 2000, almost all of my notes and records stayed behind, which means both books were written almost entirely from memory (many parts decades later) except where I could find outside material like clippings. That I remember so much, so vividly and fondly, is a testament to how well I was taught by the MIT Sloan Fellows, Kenanites, colleagues at Lucent and Bell Labs, the outstanding clients and partners, the mentors like Johnson, Wiesner, Vest, and so many others.